Pragmatic, straightforward help from an astute and expert clinician; the author draws on cutting-edge research findings to help those who suffer from the age-old problem of worry.

—Jacqueline B. Persons, Ph.D., director of the San Francisco Bay Area Center for Cognitive Therapy and associate clinical professor in the Department of Psychology at the University of California, Berkeley

DISCARDED
Richmond Public Library

This should be a welcome and helpful book for anyone whose life is disrupted by worry. LeJeune offers a practical and informative approach for dealing with worry that places it squarely in the larger and wondrous context of one's whole life! The easy-to-follow mindfulness methods and acceptance practices open the door for real transformation to any reader who actually does them.

—Jeffrey Brantley, MD, director of the Mindfulness-Based Stress Reduction Program at Duke University's Center for Integrative Medicine and author of *Calming Your Anxious Mind*

D0206918

THE WORRY TRAP

How to Free Yourself from

Worry & Anxiety

Using Acceptance &

Commitment Therapy

CHAD LEJEUNE, PH.D.

New Harbinger Publications, Inc.

Publisher's Note

This publication is designed to provide accurate and authoritative information in regard to the subject matter covered. It is sold with the understanding that the publisher is not engaged in rendering psychological, financial, legal, or other professional services. If expert assistance or counseling is needed, the services of a competent professional should be sought.

Distributed in Canada by Raincoast Books

Copyright © 2007 by Chad LeJeune
New Harbinger Publications, Inc.
5674 Shattuck Avenue
Oakland, CA 94609

Cover design by Amy Shoup; Acquired by Catharine Sutker;
Edited by Carole Honeychurch

All Rights Reserved
Printed in the United States of America

New Harbinger Publications' Web site address: www.newharbinger.com

---

Library of Congress Cataloging-in-Publication Data

LeJeune, Chad.
   The worry trap : how to free yourself from worry & anxiety using acceptance and commitment therapy / Chad LeJeune.
      p. cm.
   ISBN-13: 978-1-57224-480-1
   ISBN-10: 1-57224-480-1
   1. Anxiety—Treatment.   2. Worry—Treatment.   3. Acceptance and commitment therapy.   I. Title.
RC531L4543 2007
616.85'2206—dc22

                                                          2006039640

09   08   07

10   9   8   7   6   5   4   3   2   1

First printing

To all of the clients who have honored me by sharing their worries and their triumphs. You have been my greatest teachers.

CONTENTS

FOREWORD

The human mind evolved to prevent harm, not to promote subjective feelings of well-being, happiness, or wholeness. Fifty thousand years ago early humans were clinging precariously to a rough existence, seemingly with almost no tools to survive. They did not have big teeth like the lion or fast legs like the cheetah. They were neither as strong as the gorilla nor as well protected as the tortoise. But they had a human mind, and that made all the difference.

Using your mind to avoid harm requires the ability to do three things: to categorize, predict, and evaluate. To use our minds to solve problems we need to treat our symbols for events and their features as if they and the images they evoke are the events themselves. We can imagine difficult situations almost as if we are there, seeing the features of the situation in great detail. Then we can imagine what we might do and the results that might be produced. And finally, we can consider these results in comparison to other results that might be produced by other actions. All this through the use of symbols—we can do it all without ever leaving our chairs.

It is an amazing feat. And it gave us the edge as a species. As a result of these abilities we were able to imagine what might happen to us if we went out on the savannah. We were able to categorize the conditions in which the lion might attack or the cheetah might run us down. We were able to develop weapons, formulate plans, and test approaches that gradually put human beings in a position of relative safety. We did not have to do it simply by trial and error or by instinct. We could reason it all through.

Our basic research laboratories (those doing the work that forms a foundation for the clinical approach described in this book) are learning that these abilities are established in human children very early and that they are central to their intellectual abilities and behavioral success. But they have a dark side. These abilities, so central to our individual and collective success, evolved to prevent harm, not to promote subjective feelings of well-being. The same abilities that allow us to visualize and solve real problems can create misery if they are turned loose on every situation. The mind can exaggerate threats, construct endless "problems," or harass us into constant vigilance. In effect, this powerful weapon can turn on its owner. Even worse, it sometimes seems to have become the owner.

"Worry" originally meant to kill or strangle, and when our minds turn back on us in this way it is as if we are being strangled by reason itself. We can easily enter into a mental world that is so dominant that it seems as though all of life is a mental event. In this state, the mind has become the master.

Fortunately, we are untangling how this happens and are learning what to do about it. This book brings together the processes our research laboratories say are most helpful in bringing the mind to heel, so that we can use it instead of being used by it.

In the past we thought that the mind had to be controlled in the sense that we had to get the *content* of our minds properly arranged. It turns out that this is not true. In fact, this notion often only feeds the overextension of the mind because that very process is intensely predictive and evaluative. It is like trying to diet successfully by eating constantly so that the food in the house will go away. It cannot work because if the process is the problem, the process will not produce a solution. Now we are learning that getting in control of our minds is more a matter of learning how to let go of the illusion that symbols and the images they evoke are the events themselves. If you want peace of mind you have to learn how to peacefully step out of the noisy maelstrom of prediction and evaluation.

The Worry Trap shows you how to do that. It is very creative in combining traditional tools such as relaxation and newer tools of acceptance, mindfulness, and values. This combination works because all of these methods are harnessed to a common mission under a single, coherent model: acceptance and commitment therapy (ACT).

ACT is not so much a specific technique as an approach. ACT teaches you how to step out of your mind and start to really live. Dr.

LeJeune has presented this model in a simple, easy to follow, and comprehensive way. He gives you things to do, not just things to think about. He anticipates the objections and gently guides you through them.

This book is not about eliminating your worries so much as transforming your life. It's about putting you back in control of your life by learning how to let go of trying needlessly to control the content of that verbal organ between your ears. It's about giving up control of the uncontrollable and instead starting to really live. Now.

—Steven C. Hayes

ACKNOWLEDGMENTS

The ideas and suggestions collected here reflect the efforts of many researchers and clinicians who have worked to better understand worry, anxiety, and the other ins and outs of the human condition. This book owes its conceptual heart to Steven Hayes, who, along with Kirk Strosahl, Kelly Wilson, and others, has so openly shared his work and ideas with all of us. It is the nonproprietary and generous nature of the founders of ACT that has allowed it to help so many. My understanding of anxiety and worry also owes much to the work of David Barlow, Richard Heimberg, Susan Orsillo, and Lizabeth Roemer.

This book would never have been written without the care and trust of many people who have supported my development, both as a psychologist and as a person. Sandy Evarts, Donald Jackson, Luciana Profaca, and Felice Parisi have each played a key role over the years by offering me their confidence and sharing their expertise. Jacqueline Persons has been an exceptional teacher and mentor. My family and loved ones have offered endless encouragement and patience that goes on and on.

Many thanks to my editors at New Harbinger Publications, Catharine Sutker and Carole Honeychurch, for their belief in this project and their helpful feedback and suggestions.

Finally, I would like to acknowledge the role of my students and clients who have collectively given shape and meaning both to what I know and what I do.

WHAT IS WORRY?

WORRIED WANDA

Wanda had a lot going for her. She earned a good salary as assistant manager of a wine-storage facility. Her flexible schedule allowed her to take college courses, and she would be graduating in a few months with a bachelor's degree. Wanda was planning to take some time off and to apply to law schools over the coming year. She was engaged to a warm and caring man, Winston, whom she loved very much. Wanda had money in the bank, good health, lots of friends, and her whole life ahead of her. So why was she so miserable?

Wanda was worried. She fretted about finishing her degree. Sure, she had made it through four years of college with almost straight A's, but what if something happened in these final months and she wasn't allowed to graduate? What if there was one class that she wasn't able to pass? What if she got seriously ill or was in an accident and had to drop all of her classes? Then there was the question of law school. She wasn't sure where to apply.

Earlier in the year, she had researched so many programs and had so many options swimming around in her mind that she had finally become totally overwhelmed and decided to put off applying for another year. Winston was completely supportive, but this was a problem in itself. If she was going to be busy applying to law school next spring, getting accepted somewhere, and then moving in the summer, would they have to get married this winter? She had always imagined being married outdoors in the spring.

Would a winter wedding work as well? Would they wind up wishing they had waited?

Whenever Winston brought up scheduling the wedding, Wanda waffled. When she thought of the wedding, Wanda worried about her weight. Would she look heavy in the wedding dress she'd chosen? And what about leaving her wine warehouse job? Wanda thought her boss may kick up a fuss when Wanda quit. During the day, Wanda chewed over wide-ranging worries, while at night sleep eluded her. She even began to worry about her health. She felt tired and easily winded. Would she even be able to make it down the aisle?

WHAT IS WORRY?

While Wanda's worries may sound a bit outsized, most of us have had periods when we struggled with worry and anxiety about one or more areas of our lives. Worry is the thinking component of anxiety. Worries tend to focus on the future and anticipated problems or negative events, and they usually take the form of those "What if …" questions in our minds. Worry is not so much a response to something that is actually happening as it is a response to something that *might* happen. Since almost anything might happen, the potential for worry is virtually unlimited!

When Is Worry Excessive?

Occasional worry about major life events is common, especially during periods of transition. But for some, worry is a way of life. Like Wanda, they spend many of their waking hours thinking of all the things that could go wrong. They worry about what could happen at home, at work, to themselves, and to loved ones. Some even find that they worry about the fact that they worry so much, wondering where it all will lead. Often, this excessive worry is associated with nearly constant feelings of restlessness and anxiety. The result of all this tension can include muscle aches and pains, stomach problems, fatigue, difficulty concentrating, or trouble sleeping. If any of this sounds familiar to you, this book can help.

The Costs of Worry

People who worry a lot tend to believe that worrying helps them in some way. We will discuss these beliefs about the usefulness of worry in chapter 1, but what is known about the actual outcome of worry? While we have already mentioned some of the physical problems that can result from excessive worry, others include social, emotional, and behavioral problems. The irritability and edginess that come with frequent worry can have a negative impact on relationships at home and at work. Often worries about relationships lead to interpersonal behavior like excessive "checking in" or reassurance seeking that becomes a problem in the relationship. Frequent worry and the anxiety that accompanies it can leave you feeling emotionally depleted and depressed. For some, these problems are compounded by drinking or the use of other drugs in an attempt to turn off the worry.

Worry can also have an effect on how productive and effective you are in pursuing personal or professional goals. Individuals who worry a lot are busy thinking about possible negative events in the future. This interferes with problem solving and decision making in the present and often leads to a pattern of avoidance and procrastination. Worriers are not exactly inactive. In fact, they often engage in excessive nervous or antsy behavior. However, all this activity is often not organized or geared toward pursuing goals or addressing problems. In addition to foot tapping and pacing, other nonproductive worry behaviors include checking and rechecking to see if tasks were completed or completed accurately and going over extensive checklists again and again. Worriers often find that so much of their time and energy is expended on worrying that they have limited internal resources left over to devote to productive action. They are constantly on the move, yet they get nowhere.

HOW TO USE THIS BOOK

The Worry Trap is for anyone who is troubled by worry and wants to do something about it. The approach to worry presented here is largely based on a treatment model called acceptance and commitment therapy (ACT), developed by psychologist Steven Hayes and his colleagues. The central concepts of ACT have been organized here into a step-by-step approach to coping with worry and anxiety. Since the ideas presented build upon one another in a logical fashion, it is best to read the book in order, from start to finish, rather than skipping around.

Since many of the ideas that comprise ACT are subtle, this book is organized to offer you an experiential as well as a verbal understanding of the concepts presented. For this reason, it is important for you to do the exercises in the order in which they appear. They are designed to illustrate the concepts as they are presented and to make them real for you. Also, many of the exercises give you a chance to practice and develop skills that you will later apply during times of worry and anxiety. As always, the most effective solution to any problem is the one you are willing to carry out, so do the exercises!

You might want to buy a notebook or journal and keep it handy as you read through the book. In addition to jotting down your thoughts about what you are reading, this can be a good place to record your worry thoughts when you come to the monitoring exercises in chapter 4. When completing the exercises, you will find that some of them require you to close your eyes. Since this can make reading the instructions difficult, you may want to have someone you trust read them aloud while you complete the exercise, or else tape them on a tape recorder and then play them back.

Being open to new ideas and a change of approach always involves bravery. Even when our old ways of doing things are not working, they still have the advantage of being familiar. As such, they often feel right. Congratulations on your decision to try something new. The next chapter takes a closer look at how worry works and the problems it can cause, as well as providing an overview of what help is available. It begins with a very basic question: why worry?

CHAPTER ONE

HOW DOES WORRYING HELP YOU?

If you're reading this book, you probably have a very good idea of what worry is and how to do it, but have you ever considered why you worry? What is the purpose of worry in your life? What function does it serve? How does worrying help you?

THE USES OF WORRY

Most people who worry excessively do so because, on some level, they believe that worrying is useful in some way. As long as you believe that worrying is helpful, you may be hesitant to make any changes. Let's look at some of the ways that worry can seem to help.

Worrying as Planning and Problem Solving

One reason that people engage in frequent worry is because they confuse worrying with planning or problem solving. Since being able to plan and solve problems is essential to getting by in the world, the worrier believes that she is doing something useful and productive. Researchers have found that individuals who engage in excessive worry actually show a poorer ability to solve problems than those who worry less. This book will help you to distinguish between productive planning or problem solving on the one hand, and nonproductive worry on the other. As defined in this book, *worry* is any thought process that is associated with anxiety and is nonproductive by nature.

Worrying as a Motivator

Many worriers would respond to the question "How does worry help you?" with something like this: "Worrying helps you because it kicks your ass. It helps you to do the things that need to be done." Research, however, suggests that just the opposite is true. Many studies have shown that the process of worry is actually associated with limited and ineffective behavioral responses. Ironically, people who engage in excessive worry are more likely to procrastinate and avoid rather than engage in effective, productive activity (Borkovec, Hazlett-Stevens, and Diaz 1999). The worrier's excessive focus on the future often results in a diminished awareness of the present and is associated with poorer performance on a wide range of tasks (Metzger et al. 1990).

Worrying as Control of the Uncontrollable

Another way of understanding worry is as a primarily internal, verbal attempt to gain control over that which is essentially uncontrollable. A consistent finding in studies of chronic worriers is that, compared to others, these individuals have a low tolerance for uncertainty (Dugas et al. 1998). By focusing on the future and anticipating the worst, people who worry are attempting to reduce uncertainty by exerting an imagined control over future events. Many worriers have the superstitious belief that "If I worry about it, this will prevent it from happening." Psychologists call this "magical thinking." In chapter 4, we will take a closer look at the difference between worry on the one hand and planning and problem solving on the other. While real problem solving and planning are important and helpful, with worry, the attempt to control the future is not only imaginary but detrimental. This desire for control, while it feels like part of a solution, is all too often part of a bigger problem. The central focus of this book is to help you let go of your desire to control the uncontrollable by increasing your acceptance of the future's uncertainty and focusing on taking the necessary actions in the present to better live the life you want to live.

WORRY & ANXIETY

When we worry, we are reminding ourselves over and over again of real or imagined threats to our safety or well-being. The human body responds to any perceived threat with an automatic, hardwired response that most people identify as fear or anxiety. With frequent worry, the anticipation of problems or negative outcomes repeatedly puts the body into this crisis mode. Since worrying often does not lead to any actual activity, the increased energy and tension that result persist in the body as stress. Over time, this can lead to a number of physical problems including chronic muscle pain, high blood pressure, and a host of other stress-related illnesses. Understanding the nature of anxiety and its relationship to the desire for control that lies at the root of worry is an essential first step toward change.

The Fight-or-Flight Response

Anxiety is not only a natural part of life, it is essential for our survival as individuals and as a species. This automatic, built-in response to perceived threats allows us to take necessary action when real dangers pop up. Often called "fight-or-flight arousal," anxiety involves a series of changes in our bodies that prepare us to take immediate action to deal with a threat or crisis. The fight-or-flight response is governed by a part of the nervous system called the sympathetic nervous system. Its origins go back to a time when people lived closer to natural predators in densely forested settings.

Imagine Early Man taking a primeval stroll through his jungle neighborhood. The air is filled with sounds and smells that he is very familiar with. All of these carry their own meanings and associations for him, some comforting and others threatening. Suddenly, Early Man hears a rustling sound behind him. He turns to see a flurry of movement in the brush. Then, out of the greenery emerges a flash of orange, the dreaded saber-toothed tiger! Almost as soon as his eyes register movement, Early's brain interprets the flash of orange as "danger" and sends a message of alarm to the rest of his body. This alarm, carried by chemical messengers like adrenaline, causes several changes to occur in his body. His heart begins to beat faster and stronger, resulting in increased blood pressure. This moves blood into the large muscles of his arms (preparation to "fight") and legs (preparation for "flight"). Many of his muscle groups will tense up in anticipation of the action. Meanwhile, blood flow is diverted away from the skin surface and from the fingers and toes, which can result in paleness, tingling sensations, and "cold feet." This way, should Mr. Tiger actually sink his saber-teeth into Mr. Man, the latter is less likely to bleed to death.

Early's breathing also changes from slow breaths that originate near his abdomen to rapid breathing high in his chest. This works to get more oxygen to his muscles. Unfortunately, this type of breathing can also lead to dizziness and hot flashes, especially if he doesn't actually run anywhere. As the alarm continues to sound, Early's pupils will widen to let in more light so that he can more easily see his escape route. He will begin to sweat, which in addition to keeping him from overheating, will make him slippery and harder to catch. Finally, just in case he is thinking of having a snack before he starts to run, his whole digestive system will shut down, from the saliva glands (resulting in dry mouth) to the stomach (producing nausea or constipation).

All of these physical changes are aimed at helping our hero to either fight the tiger or to run like hell. If he does either of these, and the threat is real, the fight-or-flight response will have served him well. If the flash of orange turns out to be a harmless kitten rather than the anticipated tiger however, the fight-or-flight response will just leave him a tense, pale, constipated, sweaty mess.

Modern-Day Fight or Flight

Even though we no longer live in the forest, our bodies still respond in the same way to perceived threats. We still need this response from time to time. For example, if you are crossing the street and as you step away from the curb you notice a large bus barreling toward you, it is this response that allows you to very quickly jump back onto the curb. Instead of a speeding bus or a saber-toothed tiger, however, what if you are responding to the potential threat of missing a deadline, looking foolish in front of your boss, or forgetting to file your tax return? While the fight-or-flight response works well if you need to escape from a burning building, this same physical response is less helpful if you need to focus on writing that annual report, respond coherently to a complex question, or remember to pick up milk at the store. Since so many of the perceived threats that we encounter in modern life do not call for either fight or flight, we are often left in a state of persistent arousal with limited opportunities to release the built-up tension. If our bodies react this way often or stay in this state for extended periods of time, a variety of problems develop. Muscle aches and pains, restlessness, difficulty concentrating, persistent fatigue, sleep problems, and irritability are just a few of the problems associated with this sort of chronic overarousal.

Fight or Flight & Control

An important thing to remember about the fight-or-flight response is that it is automatic and often our very first reaction to a problem. Inherent in the response is the desire to *do something*. In this way, fight-or-flight arousal reflects an instinct to exert control over your environment. This can be useful when there is some action that needs to be taken. When this is not the case, as in nonproductive worrying, the instinct to exert control is problematic. In the next chapter, we will look more closely at the ways that control does and does not work as a response to worry.

GENERALIZED ANXIETY DISORDER

If your anxiety and worry are excessive and have continued over a long period of time, you may meet the criteria for what mental health professionals call *generalized anxiety disorder* (GAD). GAD is regarded as the most basic anxiety disorder, and studies of prevalence have found that about 5 percent of people will meet the criteria for GAD at some time in their lives. It was not until the American Psychiatric Association's publication of the fourth edition of their *Diagnostic and Statistical Manual of Mental Disorders* (DSM-IV) in 1993 that excessive and uncontrollable worry was clearly identified as the central defining feature of GAD. Since then, there has been a great deal of research on the nature of chronic worry and its treatment. According to the DSM-IV, you meet the criteria for GAD if you:

A. Experience excessive anxiety and worry more days than not for at least six months about a number of events or activities

B. Find it difficult to control the worry

C. Experience three or more of these symptoms in association with the worry:

= Restlessness or feeling keyed up or on edge

= Being easily fatigued

= Problems concentrating

= Irritability

= Muscle tension

= Sleep disturbance

In order to meet the criteria for GAD, it is also necessary that the focus of your worries not be limited to the symptoms of some other disorder (for example, only worrying about weight gain, as in anorexia, or only worrying about having a serious illness, as in hypochondriasis). In addition, the anxiety and worry or the physical symptoms must cause "clinically significant" distress or impairment in important areas of day-to-day functioning. Finally, GAD is only diagnosed if these problems are not better explained as the result of drugs or medications or of some other medical or mental condition.

When Worry Is "Generalized"

Rather than focusing on one worry topic for an extended period of time, people with GAD often move from one topic to another. It seems that when anxiety about topic A becomes intolerable, the person with GAD will escape from that anxiety by switching to worry about topic B. People with GAD may also engage in *meta-worry*, which is worry about worrying. Most individuals with GAD report that they avoid certain situations that they associate with worry. This might include social situations, separation from loved ones, or traveling. People who meet the criteria for GAD tend to visit their family doctors and medical specialists more often and are more likely to have other anxiety and mood problems, like social anxiety, panic attacks, and depression. Moreover, researchers have found that GAD is unlikely to go away on its own and is more chronic and enduring than other anxiety disorders.

A mental health diagnosis or disorder is simply a way of organizing or categorizing a specific list of symptoms. While every individual is different, through years of experience, mental health professionals often observe patterns of symptoms that seem to show up together over and over again. When this happens, the professionals get together and agree to describe a particular presentation of symptoms as a "disorder." A disorder is different from a disease, in that it can include even a temporary upset in normal functioning. Emotional or mental disorders can be viewed as existing on a continuum with less extreme emotional difficulties. Anxiety disorders involve anxiety that is more intense, lasts longer, and interferes with your life functioning more than ordinary anxiety. While you may not meet the criteria for GAD, if worry interferes with your ability to enjoy life, the ideas presented in this book will likely be helpful to you.

HELP FOR GAD & CHRONIC WORRY

As mentioned above, it is only recently that chronic worry and GAD have become a focus of treatment by mental health professionals. Over the past several years, there has been growing evidence that GAD and excessive worry can indeed be treated effectively. There are several different approaches to treatment that have been supported by scientific research in clinical settings. Most clinicians use a combination of these treatment components, which target the persistent fight-or-flight arousal of people with GAD, the specific thoughts that comprise worry, and behaviors related to worry. The various skills and concepts that you will be learning throughout this book are drawn from the following areas of clinical research.

Relaxation Training

By learning to recognize fight-or-flight arousal and to reduce the level of arousal, individuals with GAD and chronic worry can obtain some relief from the physical symptoms associated with their anxiety. Most relaxation training focuses on one of two activities: breathing and muscle relaxation. As described earlier, there are specific changes in breathing that are part of the fight-or-flight response. By learning to distinguish between the type of breathing associated with anxiety and the type of breathing that leads to relaxation, it is possible to change the way you breathe and to reduce your overall level of arousal. The same is true of muscle tension. When muscles are tense, the body as well as the brain are in crisis mode. In this state, you are more likely to anticipate problems and negative outcomes. By learning to relax your muscles at will, you send your brain the message that there is no crisis. While relaxation training can provide significant relief from the physical problems associated with chronic overarousal, these effects are very general and do not directly address the process of worry itself.

Cognitive Therapy

The specific thoughts that comprise worry are the focus of cognitive therapy, which emphasizes that it is a person's interpretations of a feared situation rather than the situation itself that determine the degree of anxiety experienced. In this form of treatment, individuals are taught to notice the specific worry thoughts that they are having and to write them down. For example, a person worried about her health might write "I have no energy lately. What if I have cancer?" This task of monitoring worry thoughts alone often results in reduced worrying. By looking at their thoughts on paper, clients experience some distance between themselves and the thoughts and often report that they find the thoughts less compelling. The process of cognitive therapy involves both therapist and client then evaluating the thoughts to determine whether or not they include distortions or logical errors. People with excessive worry often engage in two characteristic types of distorted thinking: overestimation of probability and catastrophizing.

Overestimating the probability that things will go wrong or that something bad will happen may be the most common thinking error that worriers make. For example, you might believe that it is very likely that your home will be burglarized if you forget to lock your door, even though there is a very low crime rate in your neighborhood. Similarly, many people who worry about flying believe that it is quite likely that the plane they are flying on will crash, even though they may be more likely to win the lottery than to be killed in a plane crash. Since individuals with excessive worry tend to predict events that are extremely unlikely, their belief in the protective nature of worry is often strengthened when these events fail to occur. This only acts to increase the frequency of worry.

Catastrophizing is a term used by cognitive therapists to describe worriers' tendency to anticipate extreme outcomes or to view unfortunate events as "catastrophic" and beyond their ability to cope. An example would be the mother who believes that "If my child gets a poor grade on a spelling test, he won't be able to get into a good college." Another example would be the traveler who thinks "If I miss my connecting flight, I don't know what I'll do!"

Cognitive therapists teach their clients to counter these distorted thoughts. In the case of overestimated probability, the thought is viewed as a hypothesis rather than as a fact. Clients learn to challenge the thought by reviewing all of the available evidence to determine whether or not the thought is supported by the facts. Alternative interpretations of the facts are explored. When individuals are catastrophizing, they are asked to imagine the worst-case scenario regarding their worries and then to evaluate exactly how bad this would actually be and how they might be able to cope with such an event. In addition, clients are encouraged to come up with a list of any other possible outcomes besides the worst case. Many people mistakenly view the goal of cognitive therapy as coming to see a negative event as positive or neutral. Rather, cognitive therapy is about seeing events realistically. The goal is to change the pattern of thinking from "This event will probably happen, and it will be awful! I will be devastated, and my life will never be the same!" to "This event, while unlikely to occur, would be very unpleasant. However, it would be manageable, and its effects would be time limited." While researchers have noted modest improvement in chronic worriers following cognitive therapy, many people find it very difficult to change their thoughts, even when they recognize that these thoughts are distorted or irrational. The findings of several studies of cognitive therapy have suggested that much of the benefit of this approach may lie in the process of recording and observing thoughts, thereby creating a degree of distance between thinker and thought, rather than from actually changing thoughts using cognitive techniques.

Worry Exposure

A relatively new treatment called "worry exposure" has been quite effective in changing the level of anxiety related to worrying. *Worry exposure* entails identifying the most common themes of an individual's worries and then having them practice focusing on these worries and vividly imagining the worst possible outcome related to that theme. By holding these images clearly in mind for twenty-five to thirty minutes, the individual experiences an increase in anxiety. At the end of the twenty-five to thirty minutes, the individual is allowed to think through several alternatives to the worst possible outcome. After repeating this process over and over, most people experience a decrease in the level of anxiety they feel in response to a given theme. When the thoughts associated with one theme no longer elicit much anxiety, the individual moves on to the next theme.

Worry Behavior Prevention

A related treatment component involves blocking or preventing those behaviors associated with worry. Examples of worry behavior include checking and rechecking insurance policies, calling to check on loved ones frequently, taking your temperature or checking your pulse excessively, and avoiding activities that trigger worry. These behaviors provide immediate relief from anxiety, but over time they actually act to keep worry and anxiety in our lives. If you believe that these behaviors protect you from negative outcomes and continue to do them, you never have the opportunity to test that belief and possibly change it. By preventing these worry behaviors, you have the opportunity to encounter and come to believe in the low probability of the negative outcomes these behaviors are intended to prevent.

Skill Training

Many individuals with chronic worry also lack skill in the following areas: problem solving, planning, time management, and assertiveness. Since they do not have a strategy for clearly defining problems and evaluating possible solutions, they may feel unable to cope when problems arise unexpectedly. Even when clear about a goal or direction they would like to take, many people with GAD are not able to formu-late a clear plan to move in that direction. Unable to break a seemingly monumental task down into manageable steps, worriers are over-whelmed by thoughts about goals that take the form of worry and are accompanied by anxiety. Even when a clear plan is in place, some indi-viduals with GAD have trouble sticking to the plan because they are not skilled at managing their time well. Finally, many people who spend a lot of time worrying do so because they take on too much due to difficulty saying no to others, delegating, or asking for the help they need. A number of strategies for improving your skills in all of these areas will be presented later in this book.

Acceptance & Commitment Therapy

A relatively new treatment approach developed by psychologist Steven Hayes and his colleagues, acceptance and commitment therapy (ACT) is gaining recognition as an effective treatment for a wide range of psychological problems. The evidence emerging from both mental health research and studies of basic human psychology suggests that treatment approaches that primarily emphasize change may not only be limited in their effectiveness, but may make some problems worse. A growing number of theorists and therapists are advocating a renewed focus on the importance of acceptance when dealing with difficult emotions and troubling thoughts. Acceptance and the related concept of mindfulness have been central to Eastern-based philosophy for centuries. Modern psychologists like Carl Rogers (1961) have also emphasized the transformative power of acceptance. Most recently, acceptance and commitment therapy as well as an approach called dia-lectical behavior therapy (Linehan, Kanter, and Comtois 1999) have focused on the interplay between acceptance and change. Acceptance and mindfulness-based approaches have been shown to be useful in treating anxiety, depression, substance abuse, eating disorders, trauma, couples' distress, and personality disorders.

The essential components of ACT include letting go of the struggle to control unwanted thoughts and feelings, being mindfully aware of the present moment, and committing to a course of action that is consistent with what you value most in life. In this way, ACT is about both acceptance *and* change. It is the acceptance of the thoughts and emotions that accompany a difficult but valuable act that allow you to take that action. As applied to the problem of chronic worry, your acceptance of the uncertainty of the future and your anxious thoughts and feelings about that uncertainty will allow you to focus more clearly on the present and take the steps that move you closer to the life you truly want to live.

A NEW APPROACH: HOW THIS BOOK WILL HELP YOU

This book presents a step-by-step approach that integrates the acceptance and mindfulness elements of ACT with the relaxation, thought monitoring, and exposure elements that have proven helpful for individuals with chronic worry. The next chapter lays the foundation for developing acceptance and mindfulness by focusing on what can be regarded as their opposite: the desire for control. Only by understanding the paradox of control and how it lies at the root of the process of worry can you fully grasp and apply the concepts that follow. Chapter 3 presents the basic principles of ACT. Acceptance and mindfulness are discussed as an alternative to control. While worry is a mostly verbal activity that separates us from our immediate experience, mindfulness brings us back to the present moment, giving us the opportunity to practice acceptance. With increased acceptance of our thoughts, feelings, and uncertainty, we are better able to commit to taking intentional, reasoned action. Finally, a five-step model for applying these concepts to the problem of chronic worry is presented.

Chapters 4 through 8 describe each step of the model in more detail and provide the opportunity to practice each step through exercises. Chapter 9 allows you to practice applying all of the steps together through the practice of worry exposure described earlier. The choice to engage in exposure exercises brings with it an inherent element of acceptance, making exposure an ideal way to implement and practice acceptance and mindfulness as well as commitment. Finally, in chapter 10, the skills of problem solving, planning, time management, and assertiveness are discussed with specific suggestions for improving each.

CHAPTER TWO

CONTROLLING THE UNCONTROLLABLE

One quality that worriers seem to have in common is a low tolerance for uncertainty. For all the best planning and predicting, the future remains inherently unknowable. Any thoughts beyond the present moment carry with them a high degree of uncertainty. Worry can be seen as an internal, verbal process by which we attempt (unrealistically) to reduce uncertainty by exerting imaginary control over the future. Interestingly enough, many self-help books that address the problem of chronic worry focus on developing increased control over one's worry-oriented thoughts. A review of the table of contents of these books reveals such chapter titles as "The Basic Steps of Worry Control," "Thought Stopping," "Self-Control Desensitization," and "Changing Your Physical State to Change Your Mental State." Unfortunately, this emphasis on controlling one's thoughts and feelings may actually contribute more to the problem of worry than it does to a solution. Not only is it extremely difficult to change or control thoughts or emotions, but this desire for control lies at the very root of worry itself.

THE CONTROL INSTINCT

Human beings are addicted to control. One reason for this is that we have such very large and sophisticated brains. Our big brains have allowed us, in most cases, to exert an amazing degree of control over our environment. For example, look at the downtown area of any major city. Everything you see there is a testament to man's ability to control and shape his surroundings. There is virtually nothing that exists in such an urban setting that was not conceived of and designed by human brains and produced by human hands. It should therefore come as no surprise that, as a species, one of our first instincts when confronted with an experience that we do not like is to somehow control that experience.

This "control instinct" pops up automatically and without our even noticing it all the time. In most cases, it works very well for us. For example, suppose a sudden breeze were to flip the pages of this book. You would very likely turn the pages back to this one and hold onto the book more tightly. This is the control instinct at work—and working well. If you spill a glass of water, you exert control by getting a towel and wiping up the spill. If you find that it's too warm in that wool sweater, you take it off. If you're bothered by the glare from the sun, you raise a hand to shield your eyes. In countless ways, every day, all day long, we are exercising control. Our primary operating principle could be summed up as "if you don't like it, get rid of it."

THE PARADOX OF CONTROL

While control works for us most of the time, there are certain situations where the principle of "if you don't like it, get rid of it" does not seem to apply.

A Little Experiment

Suppose you are volunteering to participate in an experiment studying people who worry. You show up at the university clinic and complete a questionnaire that asks you to identify what you have been most worried about recently. Topping your list are a number of worries about whether the new job you recently started is going to work out. After completing the questionnaire, you are shown into the laboratory where the researcher begins to attach electrodes to your temples, a blood pressure cuff to your arm, and heat sensors to your fingertips. You are informed that, in this study, the researcher will be looking at the relationship between worry and physical indicators of anxiety. The sensors attached to your body will feed information about your heart rate, blood pressure, muscle tension, and skin temperature (all parts of the fight-or-flight response) into a machine that will indicate your level of anxiety on a dial that goes from 0 to 100.

Once you are all hooked up, the researcher says, "Before we can begin, I need to ask you to lower your anxiety as much as possible. Right now your anxiety is at 40. This is much too high for us to begin the study. You'll have to get your anxiety down to at least 10 before we can even start." The researcher then turns to look at the dial, and taps his foot expectantly.

What do you think is likely to happen to your anxiety level as the researcher waits for it to go down? Will it go up, down, or remain the same? Let's suppose it goes up to 60. Now the researcher looks at you again and says something like "You know, we really don't have all day here. There are other volunteers waiting for their turn. I'm going to have to ask you to try a little bit harder. In fact, I'm only going to give you two more minutes to reduce your anxiety, and then we'll have to take more drastic measures to get you to relax!" Which way do you suppose the needle on the dial would move?

Let's say the dial is now at 80. The researcher begins to perspire and gets red in the face. He looks at you menacingly and says, "You don't seem to understand. I need this data before I can complete my dissertation. I need to complete my dissertation before I can get out of graduate school. And I *need* to get out of graduate school before I lose my mind!" At this point, the researcher pulls a large hypodermic needle from the folds of his white lab coat and holds it in front of your face. As he taps the syringe with his finger, he says, "If you can't relax on your own, this injection at the base of your skull should be helpful." What do you suppose would happen to your level of anxiety at this point? Would it start to go down? This is the paradox of control.

Control of Feelings

While control works for us in many, many situations, when we are dealing with emotions like anxiety, control seems to have the opposite of the desired effect. The harder you try to control or get rid of your anxiety, the more anxiety you seem to have. Instead of "if you don't like it, get rid of it," the principle that seems to apply here is "if you try to get rid of it, you're going to have more of it." One way of understanding why is to consider the instinctive nature of both control and fight-or-flight arousal as a response to threatening situations. Fight-or-flight arousal helps us to get ready to control a situation. The paradox is that when the situation we are trying to control is anxiety (or anger, or stress, or other "undesirable" feelings), this response in itself produces more of the unwanted feeling.

To distinguish between the anxiety that we feel in a situation and the additional anxiety that results when we try to get rid of that anxiety, psychologist Steven Hayes and his colleagues coined the terms "clean anxiety" and "dirty anxiety" (1993). Remember your initial readout of 40 on the researcher's anxiety dial? This is the level of anxiety that you felt at that moment, being hooked up to an unfamiliar machine and participating in a research study. This would be your "clean anxiety." When you tried to reduce your anxiety in response to the researcher's instructions and threats, the increase in your anxiety level to 60 then 80 is comprised of "dirty anxiety." In other words, clean anxiety is that anxiety which arises in response to a particular situation. Dirty anxiety is anxiety *about* this initial anxiety. What do you think would have happened to your anxiety if the researcher had been fine with the initial readout of 40? If you were fully accepting of an anxiety level of 40, do you think that level would have increased? Might it have eventually gone down? It seems that when we are able to accept the clean anxiety that we have in response to a given situation and let go of any attempt to control or get rid of that anxiety, the result is the absence of the dirty anxiety related to our control response.

Control of Thoughts

This example highlights the effects of the control instinct when we are dealing with emotions. But what about thoughts? Let's return to the laboratory and our earnest researcher. Remember that questionnaire you completed and your worries about the new job? Suppose the researcher says, "In order to begin the study, it's very important that you start by not thinking about your new job at all. Clear your mind of any thoughts about the job, what's expected of you in this job, what your boss might be thinking of you, or what might happen if you aren't able to cut it. Don't think about whether or not you might lose the job or decide to quit or what it would be like to have to look for a job." Turning to the dial, the researcher says, "Okay, when you have successfully stopped thinking about your job, raise your hand."

How well would this work? What would happen to your ability to stop thinking about the job as the incentive to do so increased? Most people find that the more they want to avoid thinking about something, the more likely they are to think about that very thing. In fact, it is only when we decide that "I must not think about X" that we begin to experience thoughts about X as intrusive and pervasive. The stronger the prohibitions against a thought, the more out of our control the thought seems to be. Most of us have experienced this in social situations when we have told ourselves: "Don't look at the pimple on his nose" or "Don't think about that bit of spinach between her teeth." Inevitably, this "forbidden" detail becomes the only thing we can focus on. In some cases, when thoughts are especially disturbing and we believe that we absolutely, positively *must not* think them, these thoughts become obsessions. Consider the case of Irwin.

Irwin's Dangerous Thought

As a proud father and successful provider, Irwin understood the importance of maintaining proper control at all times. As head of the accounting department for a large corporation, he had reaped the rewards of years of discipline and organization. For this reason, Irwin was more than a little disturbed when a random thought caught him by surprise on a late Sunday afternoon as he sat behind the wheel of his family's Range Rover. The family had been on an outing in the country and were returning to the city along a curving two-lane highway. Irwin's wife sat next to him, and his two small daughters were both asleep in the backseat. Suddenly, as a car rounded the curve ahead and was approaching in the opposite lane, a thought popped into Irwin's head: "If I just turned the wheel a little to the left, we would all be killed instantly." Well, Irwin was startled by this thought, to say the least. Somehow, it didn't seem like the sort of thought a responsible and loving father should have. Irwin's next thought went something like this: "I must not think that thought that I just thought. I must force such thoughts out of my mind. That thought is dangerous and has no business being in my head!" Irwin noticed himself growing tense. His heart beat faster in his chest, and he tightened his grip on the steering wheel.

However, when another oncoming car came into view, there was the thought, sitting right in the front of his mind: "If I just turned the wheel a little to the left, we would all be killed instantly." Irwin was shocked! Why wouldn't this thought go away? Did he secretly want to kill himself? His family? What if this alien and dangerous thought were to take over? Irwin felt a growing surge of anxiety as his palms began to sweat, and his face grew flushed. At the next curve, he pulled over onto the shoulder of the road. Turning to his wife, he explained that he was feeling tired from all the driving and would really appreciate it if she could drive the rest of the way home.

Irwin's case illustrates what can happen when we regard thoughts as dangerous or threatening, and moreover, what can happen when we decide that we must not have those thoughts. As it turns out, the specific thought that popped into Irwin's head while driving down that two-lane road is not an uncommon thought for a driver to have. If you take an informal poll, you will likely find that many people have had similar thoughts when driving in similar situations. While most people would agree that this is an unpleasant thought and would not choose to linger on it, most people are not as shocked and frightened by the thought as Irwin was. It's only a thought, after all. While the physical act of turning the steering wheel to the left would be very dangerous, the thought of doing so is not dangerous at all. Contrary to Irwin's fears, thoughts do not take control of people's actions and force them to do things they do not want to do. If Irwin had continued to drive, he would have discovered that while he may not have had control of the thoughts that popped into his mind, he would have continued to have control of his behavior. Unfortunately, Irwin chose to pull over and let his wife drive. He most likely did this in an effort to gain control or to get rid of the unwanted thoughts and the associated anxiety.

While this may work in the short term, the problem for Irwin is that his choice to stop driving supports his belief that his thoughts are dangerous. He might come to believe that the only reason he and his family were not killed by these dangerous thoughts is because he let his wife drive. While he may have the immediate sense of controlling his anxiety with the avoidant response of letting his wife drive, if he continues to avoid driving when his family is in the car, he will likely find that his anxiety is controlling *him*.

Cognitive Fusion

One reason that people often become so frightened and disturbed by their thoughts is that they actually confuse thoughts about a certain event with the event itself. For Irwin, the thought of a head-on collision was as frightening as an actual head-on collision and elicited the same fight-or-flight response. Acceptance and commitment therapy provides a term for this tendency to equate thoughts with the things or events that they refer to. The term is *cognitive fusion*, and it suggests the "fusion" of the thought with the actual real-life event or experience that the thought references (Hayes, Strosahl, and Wilson 1999). For example, an ACT therapist would describe Irwin's problem as a fusion of the thought of having a head-on collision with the actual experience of a collision. He is only experiencing the thought of a collision, but he is reacting as though he were experiencing the actual collision. People who worry excessively often experience as much anxiety in response to thoughts about anticipated events as they would to the events themselves. For example, a husband who has a disagreement with his wife might have the thought "what if she divorces me?" and imagine a scenario in which his wife becomes so angry that she decides to end their marriage. While these are only thoughts and refer to events that may in fact be very unlikely, during the course of a day of worrying the husband might feel all of the same emotions he would experience if he were in fact going through a divorce. An essential part of accepting our thoughts is recognizing that they are separate from the events they refer to. In ACT, this process is called *cognitive defusion* (Hayes et al. 2004). The exercises presented in chapter 6 will help you to develop this separation of thoughts from actual events.

Control and the Outside/Inside Principle

From these examples, we begin to see that while control is a very useful and adaptive response when dealing with any number of situations in the outside world, when it comes to inside experiences like feelings and thoughts, the control response turns out to be more of a problem than a solution. In other words, when we are dealing with events on the *outside*, the rule seems to be "if you don't like it, get rid of it." When we are dealing with our experience on the *inside*, however, the rule that applies is "if you try to get rid of it, you end up with more of it."

Understanding this outside/inside principle has important implications for people who worry excessively. Since worry is an experience that mostly happens on the inside, taking the approach of "I'm just not going to worry about that" or following the common advice to "try not to worry about it" is likely to result in only one thing: more worry. While trying to control our inside experiences like worry and anxiety tends not to work, taking control remains a useful strategy for many situations on the outside. Learning to distinguish between those elements of our experience where control is likely to be helpful (outside) and those where it tends to be counterproductive (inside) is a major focus of this book. The relationship between inside and outside is reflected in the name of acceptance and commitment therapy. By accepting our experience on the inside, we are better able to commit to purposeful action on the outside.

The Wrinkle in Your Sock

Feelings like anxiety and thoughts like worry thoughts are a little like a wrinkle in your sock. You have probably had the experience of walking down the sidewalk and feeling a small wrinkle in your sock. This little lumping of extra fabric trapped between your foot and your shoe can create a slightly uncomfortable pressure as you walk, like something soft stuck in your shoe. Sometimes you can get rid of the wrinkle with just a wiggle of your toes. Other times, reaching down and pulling up your sock does the trick. Occasionally, you might have to actually stop walking, sit down, remove your shoe, and completely readjust your sock before you can continue. Now, imagine what it would be like if you had an absolute zero tolerance for even the smallest wrinkle in your socks. What if you were not willing to have the slightest hint of a wrinkle and spent much of the day working to keep your socks pulled up tight and snug. When you walk down the sidewalk, you stop after every tenth step, bend down, and tug at your sock. At least once in every block, you have to plop down on the curb, take off your shoe, and make an adjustment. Because of this, you are almost always late to appointments. You show up late for that important meeting at work, wriggling your toes and bending over to tug at your sock as you hobble to your chair, apologizing to your colleagues. You try to pay attention to what your boss is saying but find that you are distracted by what feels like yet another wrinkle in your sock. Pulling your chair away from the table, you raise one leg up and heave your foot onto the table.

Your boss stops talking, and everyone at the table looks at you and your foot. Unlacing your shoe for the hundredth time that day, you again apologize, but explain to your coworkers that you have this "darn wrinkle" that you need to get rid of. For the sake of thoroughness, you actually take your sock all the way off this time and start from the beginning, pulling it on slowly and smoothing away any wrinkles as you go. Later, after being offered some surprise time off by your boss, you are driving home only to be pulled over by a traffic patrol officer. The officer explains that you were careening all over the road. She is less than understanding when you explain that you were trying to sort out a wrinkle that was "right down near the ball" of your foot, and that you only had your leg sticking out the window so that you could fully flex your foot while pulling on the top of your sock. Can you imagine all of this?

Suppose the most important thing for you, once there was a wrinkle in your sock, was to get rid of it. You might complain that these wrinkles in your sock were a serious interference in your daily functioning. Upon seeing a therapist, you might even say something like "These darn wrinkles are ruining my life!" Would this be true? Would it be the wrinkles themselves that were the cause of your impairment? In this scenario, what is it exactly that interferes with your daily functioning? Would it be correct to say that it is not the wrinkles so much as the lack of willingness to have wrinkles that is a problem? What would your life be like if you were willing to occasionally have a small wrinkle in your sock and were still able to continue on your way? Efforts to get rid of worry and anxiety are like spending all of your time trying to adjust your sock. The effort to control your thoughts and feelings (to get the wrinkles out) is likely to cause more problems for you than the worry-provoking situation itself (the wrinkles).

CONTROL IS UBIQUITOUS: A CAUTIONARY INTERLUDE

Before moving on to the "how to" section of this book, take a moment to appreciate the significance of what you have read so far. While this chapter on control is fairly abstract compared to the remaining chapters, the concepts here are essential to all that follows. You may be thinking to yourself, "Okay, I get it. Control—bad; acceptance—good. Now let's move on." However, it is important to grasp that the desire to control is not only very strong, it is instinctual and automatic. It is our *primary* response. We spend much of our lives learning to control things. In many ways, control seems to be what human beings are specially adapted to do. Since this response is so ubiquitous, before we can hope to let go of it, we must first be able to recognize it when it occurs.

For example, as you have been reading this, you may have noticed the slightest urge to hurry through this chapter to get on to chapter 3 and chapter 4. You might have thought, "Okay, okay. I understand these concepts; now let's get on to the part that tells me what to *do* to get rid of this worry problem!"

Does this sound at all familiar? How else might we describe this desire to skip ahead? This urge to hurry on to the next chapter is an excellent example of the desire for control. Did you catch that? Did you notice that it was happening even as you were reading this chapter on control? All of the ideas that follow in this book build upon the understanding that control is part of the problem of worry, not part of the solution. For that reason, this chapter is very important. In addition, this chapter is all the more important because it's the one that you're reading *right now*. So, read it carefully. And, if necessary, read it twice.

CONTROL AS CONTEXT: GETTING THE BIGGER PICTURE

Control is so central to how we operate as human beings that it is more than just one specific response to a given situation; it is more like a system or context that we bring to all of our experiences.

The Person in the Hole

Therapists trained in acceptance and commitment therapy use a number of metaphors with their clients to highlight the ubiquitous nature of the control response and the many ways that control does not work when dealing with problems like anxiety and worry. A favorite is the person-in-the-hole metaphor described by Steven Hayes and his colleagues (1999). In this metaphor, the person with a problem is compared to a person in a hole. When we are faced with problems to which we see no apparent solution, it can often feel like being trapped at the bottom of a deep hole. The person who finds himself in a hole often feels a strong urge to do something about the problem. Looking desperately about, the person in the hole spies a shovel. "Thank God!" he exclaims, "A shovel!" and begins to dig furiously, straight down.

Do you see any problem with this response? The person in the hole doesn't. He has a problem, and he is doing something about it. The shovel is the only tool available. He knows how to use a shovel, and he's using it! When we are faced with problems of the inside variety, like anxiety and worry, and we respond with control, we are like the person in the hole. Control is our shovel. The control response, which works so well for us in so many situations and which is so instinctual and automatic, makes as much sense to us as digging does to the person in the hole. And, like the person in the hole, what appears to be part of the solution (control/digging) is actually part of the problem.

Remember the rule that applies to our inside experiences? If you try to get rid of it, you end up with more of it. Trying to get rid of worry and anxiety is like digging when you're in a hole. There are probably many different things that you have tried to get rid of these uncomfortable feelings and thoughts. Reading this book may even be one of them. Reading this book to learn how to get rid of anxiety and worry, however, is like the person in the hole looking around for a bigger and better shovel. Of course, having gained this insight, you might read the subsequent chapters in search of a ladder rather than a shovel. However, if the goal is still to get rid of or control your feelings and thoughts, you're using that ladder to dig ... straight down. When this happens, it's because digging is more than just a response. It's your entire operating system.

Control is so basic to human experience that it often becomes more than just a specific response to specific problems. Control can become the way we operate in life. Much like the operating system on a computer, this system of control becomes the context in which we experience thoughts and emotions. Just as the operating system on a personal computer (for example, the Windows operating system) determines how documents and images appear on the screen, this operating system of control colors our experience of thoughts and emotions. Since the control response to anxiety and worry is to get rid of them, we experience them in a context of not being willing to have them. This book is about developing a new operating system or a new context for these feelings. The word we will use for this context is *willingness*. It is important to realize that until now you may not have ever experienced anxiety or worry in the context of being willing to have these experiences. Experiencing these same thoughts and emotions but in a different context is called a *contextual shift*, and it changes our overall experience. Steven Hayes and his colleagues (1993) point to the story of the man in the gas tank to illustrate the importance of context.

The Man in the Gas Tank

Once upon a time, there was a man who lived in a gas tank. It was a big gas tank with only a little gas, but it had lots of fumes and all of the comforts of home. The man in the gas tank lived next door to a woman who lived in a water tank. The water tank was not completely dry, but it was cozy enough. Being good friends, the two frequently dined together. Enjoying his coffee after one of these dinners, the man in the gas tank was admiring the warm glow made by the candles that adorned the little table of the woman in the water tank. He thought reproachfully of how dinners in his gas tank were always dark and gloomy by comparison and determined that he would serve his next dinner by candlelight as well. The following week, the man in the gas tank made a point of buying candles and matches when he did his shopping. Hurrying home, he arranged the candles on his table, and just to see how much they would add to the ambiance, he decided to light them as well. Unfortunately, there was a big explosion. The end.

The moral of the story: context is vital.

To see how context shapes experience, consider the following question: what caused the explosion in the story? If your response is "the match," you should know that these were the very same matches purchased by the woman in the water tank. She lit matches all day and all night and never had a problem with explosions. So, the match is hardly to blame. Was it the fumes in the gas tank that caused the explosion? The man in the gas tank would have begged to differ. He had lived in that gas tank with those very same fumes for a number of years. He may have become a tad light-headed on occasion, but in all that time, he never had a problem with explosions. So, if it wasn't the match, and it wasn't the fumes, what caused the explosion?

The answer, of course, is that it is the matches *in the context of* the gas tank that resulted in an explosion. Context changes everything. When we experience an emotion like anxiety, that's the match. It is only when we experience this emotion in the context of a desire to control or eliminate anxiety that we get an explosion. Experiencing anxiety and worry in a context of willingness to have those experiences is like lighting the match outside of the gas tank. You still have the feelings and thoughts, but no explosions. In the next chapter we will begin to look at what this context of willingness looks like and how this book can help you to develop this new "operating system," which can change your overall experience of worry and anxiety.

CHAPTER THREE

ACCEPTANCE, COMMITMENT, & WILLINGNESS

If control is central to the problem of excessive worry and anxiety, what is the alternative to control? The short answer to this question is "willingness." This chapter provides a closer look at the concept of willingness and how it relates to the goals of acceptance and commitment. Then, it provides an overview of how to actually put these concepts to work when you're faced with anxiety and worry.

WILLINGNESS & THE OUTSIDE/INSIDE PRINCIPLE

We can develop willingness in two areas of experience: outside and inside.

Outside Willingness = Commitment

Willingness on the outside involves a willingness to *do* the things that are important or valuable to us. This willingness on the outside can be described as a commitment to take action in a specific way. Of course, taking certain actions is often associated with certain feelings and thoughts. When it comes to taking action in areas where we tend to avoid and procrastinate, these feelings and thoughts often include anxiety and worry.

Inside Willingness = Acceptance

Willingness on the inside means a willingness to *feel* the feelings and *experience* the thoughts that come up in a given situation or when we take a specific action. We are most willing to take action when we are willing to have the feelings and thoughts associated with that action.

Acceptance + Commitment = Willingness

Inside and outside willingness work together. As we become more accepting of our thoughts and feelings (inside), we are more willing to take action (outside). Likewise, increasing our commitment to action (outside) brings with it an inherent degree of acceptance (inside). This book will focus on increasing all-around willingness by helping you to develop both more acceptance of anxiety and worry and more commitment to taking action. In developing your willingness to feel, think, and experience (acceptance) and your willingness to act (commitment) as an alternative response to worry and anxiety, you are creating a context of willingness (as opposed to one of control) in which to experience anxious feelings and worrisome thoughts.

THE PASSENGERS ON THE BUS

To further illustrate these concepts of acceptance, commitment, and willingness, it helps to borrow yet another metaphor from Steven Hayes and his colleagues (1999). According to this metaphor, when you consider what is most important to you in life, the things you want to do, and the direction in which you want to move, you are like a bus driver committed to a specific route. There are scheduled stops along the route. These are the things you are committed to doing that move you along in the desired direction. At each of these stops, different passengers get on the bus. These passengers are the thoughts and feelings associated with that stop. Some of these passengers you are happy to see. Others, however, you would just as soon not have on your bus. These are the passengers with bad body odor or who look threatening in some way. For example, when you come to the bus stop marked "starting a new job," a number of unpleasant passengers get on. Some of them are thoughts like "What if I screw up really bad?" or "What if I can't get along with my new boss?" Other passengers are feelings, like "Mr. Anxiety" or "Miss Dread." These passengers are rowdy and distracting.

One way of responding when they get on your bus is to pull over to the side of the road, stop the bus, set the parking brake, and try to kick them off. The problem with this response is that you might spend hours fighting with these thoughts and feelings. All this time, your bus is going absolutely nowhere. What's more, even if you are successful after a great deal of effort in throwing these unwanted passengers off the bus, guess who's going to be waiting to get on at the next stop? This effort to toss unwanted thoughts and feelings off the bus is the control response. It's exhausting, and it doesn't work in the long run.

There's another way that you sometimes respond to these passengers. Sometimes, you change your plans and even the direction in which you are driving to avoid picking them up. When one of these undesirable thoughts or feelings does manage to get on the bus, you make a deal with it. If Mr. Anxiety agrees to settle down at the very back of the bus and keep a low profile, you'll go wherever he wants you to go. So, instead of driving straight down Main Street as planned, you turn left at the next corner. This is the strategy of avoidance and procrastination. You take the detour, and for a while the passengers keep quiet. Mr. Anxiety stays out of sight. If you try to get back on the main road, however, he stands up and threatens to come to the front of the bus. That's when you slow down and take another side road, just to keep him at bay.

This metaphor raises a number of questions. First, you're the one driving the bus, but who's in control of where it goes? Are you avoiding and procrastinating to maintain control of your thoughts and feelings? Or are your thoughts and feelings controlling you?

If you are the bus driver in this metaphor, how are you ever going to get down Main Street? What will allow you to move your life in the direction you truly value and choose? Control doesn't work. That response leaves you spending most of your time and energy parked on the side of the road, fighting with your thoughts and feelings. Procrastination and avoidance don't work and in fact move you further away from your goals, leaving you stuck on the bus at the mercy of the thoughts and feelings that you are trying to keep at bay.

Once again, the answer is willingness. What would happen if you were able to just make room for these undesirable passengers on your bus? What if you could accept the anxiety and worry, letting it board the bus and sit anywhere it wanted to? Doing this would mean that instead of fighting with these passengers or making deals with them, you could keep your eyes on the road and your hands on the wheel. You would be committed to sticking to your scheduled route. By accepting your thoughts and feelings, you would be able to commit to making all of the scheduled stops. You would be willing to act, as well as to think, feel, and experience whatever got onto the bus along the way.

WILLINGNESS VS. WANTING

It's important to make the distinction here between being *willing* to experience anxiety and worry and *wanting* these experiences. The phrase "embrace those feelings" has not only become a cliché, it's misleading. No one is suggesting that you hug those smelly passengers on the bus or that you seek them out. Being willing to experience your thoughts and feelings does not mean that you have to like them or want them—it simply means that you are willing to make room for them. Have you ever had the experience of allowing a guest into your home, even though you did not really want that person to be there? Think of anxiety and worry as the in-laws that you are less than happy to see, but that you manage to make welcome anyway. Why would you do this? Because it works to do so. In the case of the in-laws, making room for them works for your marriage and is better than the scene that would result if you threw them out of the house. In the case of thoughts and feelings, making room for them works in that it allows you to do the things that are important to you and is better than the escalating "dirty" anxiety that results when you are not willing to feel what you feel.

ACCEPTANCE VS. GIVING UP

Finally, all this talk about acceptance does not mean that your problems with anxiety and worry are beyond hope and you should just accept being miserable. Accepting your anxious feelings and worry-oriented thoughts is not the same as accepting feeling miserable. Remember, it is not the anxiety or worry themselves that make you miserable but your relationship to them (the context in which you experience them). Far from giving up, acceptance and commitment allow you to move on.

WHAT TO DO WHEN WORRYING STARTS

At this point, you may be on board with the goal of acceptance (at least in theory) but wondering how to begin to accept the thoughts and feelings that you have always experienced as so upsetting. Putting the somewhat abstract concepts of acceptance, commitment, and willingness into practice when we are faced with anxiety and worry can be challenging. The following five-step model can help you to interrupt the control response and become more accepting of your thoughts and feelings while also becoming more focused on the present moment and committing to taking the actions that move you in the right direction. The five steps can be applied sequentially in the moments when you first become aware that you are worrying. To make it easier to remember, the five steps are all contained in the acronym LLAMP:

Label "worry thoughts"

Let go of control

Accept and observe thoughts and feelings

Mindfulness of the present moment

Proceed in the right direction

In the chapters that follow, you will have the opportunity to practice and develop each of these steps as an individual skill. In practice, however, all of the steps work together as a unified approach to worry and anxiety. With practice, the steps will begin to flow, one into another, so that applying LLAMP becomes a fluid process. Labeling certain thoughts as "worry" is a cue to Let go of the control response, which makes room for Acceptance and Mindfulness (which work together) of thoughts, feelings, and experiences in the present moment, which then allows us to **P**roceed with valued, purposeful action. Here's a brief overview of exactly what is involved in each step.

Labeling: When to Turn On the LLAMP

In order to get the full benefit of the LLAMP approach, it is important to know when to apply it. It's likely that you often step into the worry trap without realizing it. At times, your worry may be so automatic that you are not even aware of the worry thoughts until you have worked yourself up to an uncomfortable level of anxiety. At other times, you may believe that you are engaged in planning or problem solving when you are actually worrying. Being able to apply this first step of identifying and labeling certain thoughts as worry involves two processes: First, raising your awareness of what your thoughts are and second, learning to identify thoughts that are nonproductive and label them as "worry." Just the process of noticing and labeling thoughts as worry often provides a degree of relief for excessive worriers.

This labeling step is essentially the thought-monitoring component of cognitive therapy discussed in chapter 1 that has been found to be helpful for individuals with chronic worry. By labeling thoughts in this way, you gain distance from them, drawing a distinction between yourself and your thoughts. This prepares you for practicing the acceptance and mindfulness steps that come later. In the context of the LLAMP approach, instead of struggling to change these thoughts, labeling them as worry is the first step toward letting go of the struggle. Becoming more aware of what tends to trigger worry, associated feelings and bodily sensations, and the way you respond behaviorally to worry will also help you to identify and label worry when it occurs.

Letting-Go Exercises

As described in the first two chapters, our initial, instinctual response when confronted with a problem or threat includes fight-or-flight arousal and an associated desire to control, fix, or get rid of the problem. The fight-or-flight response prepares us to take control. In order to make room for willingness as a response to worry and anxiety, we must first let go of this control response. This is the prerequisite step of letting go of the shovel when we are in the hole. Since the fight-or-flight response is associated with "digging" or controlling, relaxing this response somewhat can prepare the way for practicing acceptance and mindfulness. This book will teach you several letting-go exercises that can help with the transition from the initial control response to acceptance. Therapists who treat anxiety and worry typically include many of these exercises in their treatment plans. Among other things, they can sometimes provide temporary relief from the chronic muscle tension that people with GAD often experience. In the context of the LLAMP approach, however, it is important to remember that these letting-go exercises are not tools to get rid of anxiety. Remember the paradox of control described in the last chapter. Using these exercises to let go of anxiety and worry is likely to be of limited use. Rather, the goal is to let go of the control response itself—metaphorically speaking, to let go of the shovel. Rather than helping you to let go of anxiety, these exercises will help you to let go and *feel* anxiety or whatever else you may be feeling.

Acceptance: Making Room for What's Already There

The next step is to not only observe, but to say hello to the worry and anxiety that you have just become aware of. The ability to practice acceptance of your thoughts and feelings is something that develops over time. Acceptance works together with the next step, mindfulness, and practicing one helps to develop the other. The chapter on acceptance emphasizes two concepts. The first is that you are bigger than and separate from your worries. As you are better able to separate your self from your thoughts, feelings, and experiences, you will grow to be more accepting of whatever it may be that you as the observer are observing.

The second concept you'll learn is the separate nature of thoughts and the things, people, and events that they refer to. This idea is referred to as cognitive defusion in the language of ACT. The acceptance step is a subtle one, and explaining exactly how to do it is much like trying to tell someone how to whistle. Saying "purse your lips and blow" doesn't quite capture it. Simply observing your thoughts, feelings, and sensations, however, is a good place to start. This chapter includes a number of exercises to help you begin to experience the separation of self from experience and of thoughts from what they refer to (their *referents*).

Mindfulness: The Opportunity to Think/Feel/Experience

You can think of mindfulness as the "technology" for developing acceptance and willingness. Accepting our thoughts and feelings means being aware of them. Mindfulness involves being aware of and open to everything that we are experiencing at a given moment in time, observing our experience in a compassionate, nonjudgmental way. Mindfulness can involve observing our thoughts, our feelings, and our sensory experiences.

While the process of worry takes us out of the present by focusing on the future, mindfulness brings us back to the present moment. We actually begin practicing mindfulness with the first LLAMP step of labeling our thoughts. The step of accepting our thoughts and feelings also involves mindfulness. In the mindfulness step of LLAMP, we expand that awareness and acceptance to include not only our thoughts and feelings but all aspects of our experience in the present moment. Becoming more firmly rooted in the present sets the stage for the final step of the LLAMP approach. In chapter 7, we will look at a number of ways to develop and practice mindfulness in your daily life.

Proceed: Willingness to Act

As mentioned in the first chapter, people who worry excessively often respond to anxiety with avoidance and procrastination. At other times, they believe that until they have resolved all of their reservations and doubts about certain aspects of their lives it's impossible to take action. Sometimes their low tolerance for uncertainty leaves them feeling directionless and paralyzed when it comes to taking even the first steps. Proceeding is the commitment component of acceptance and commitment therapy, and involves choosing a direction, committing to specific actions, and following through with those actions. A direction is different from a goal in that it guides our choices even as our specific goals change. The direction that we choose is guided by our values.

This step involves developing clarity about what we value most in life and allowing these values to serve as a compass, pointing us in the right direction. It also involves being honest about what course of action is most consistent with our values and being willing to take action even as we think, feel, and experience all that goes along with a given choice. Chapter 8 will help you to clarify what it is that you value most in life and make the distinction between worrying about life and loved ones and caring for your life and for your loved ones through value-guided action.

LLAMP AND THE OUTSIDE/INSIDE PRINCIPLE

Remember, your goal in applying the LLAMP approach to worry and anxiety is to develop overall willingness. Willingness on the inside means a willingness to think, feel, and experience all of your thoughts, feelings, and sensations. This is the acceptance part of the equation and will be put into practice through the first four steps: label, let go, accept, and mindfulness. Willingness on the outside means willingness to take action. This is the commitment part of the equation, the final step of proceeding in the right direction.

Figure 3.1 describes the process of worry. It usually starts with some sort of trigger on the outside. Inside, the thoughts, feelings, and sensations related to worry include specific worries, anxiety, and associated bodily sensations like tension, racing heartbeat, or upset stomach. Typically, people who worry excessively respond on the outside with avoidance, procrastination, and other worry behavior. In the next chapter, you will begin to identify your own worry triggers, as well as the specific thoughts, feelings, and sensations that you experience as worry. Finally, you will learn to notice your own worry behavior when it occurs. This will help you to apply the LLAMP steps, inside and outside, as pictured in figure 3.2.

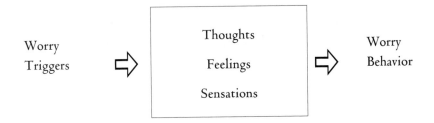

Figure 3.1: The Worry Process: Outside and Inside

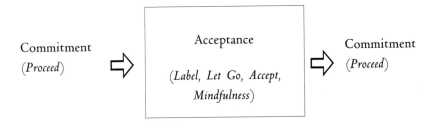

Figure 3.2: Acceptance and Commitment: Outside and Inside

CHAPTER FOUR

LABEL YOUR WORRY THOUGHTS

How often do you engage in thinking? How often during your waking hours does your mind actively process information and provide you with thoughts? Whether we realize it or not, the correct answer to this question, for everyone, is the same: once a day, every day, all day long. People think. That's just what they do. And they do it *all the time*. You're doing it right now. Of course, as you're reading these words, you are thinking about the meaning behind them and the message that they convey collectively, but you are also thinking about other things. You may be thinking about what time it is or whether you're comfortable reading in this position. You might be thinking that you are too warm or too cold or that it might be time for a little snack. You might be asking yourself questions like whether you will have time to finish this chapter now or will have to come back to it later, whether or not the ideas in this book can help you, or what you might find in the refrigerator if you were to search out that little snack. You might even be worrying about something in another part of your mind even as you are reading this book about worry. We never take a break from this thinking process. Even when we space out and, if asked, would say that, we are thinking about "nothing," we are thinking about something.

When people meditate, they may think about their breathing or the sound of a mantra that they repeat over and over, or they may quietly observe whatever thoughts pass through their minds—but they are still thinking. The mind is like a river that flows on and on, continuously, as long as we are alive. The thoughts keep coming, one after another, whether we are paying attention to them or not.

We spend so much time thinking that we are often not at all aware of *what* we are thinking. Our thoughts are so automatic and continuous that we often fail to notice them at all, like the sound of a refrigerator running or the faint sensation of our heart beating. When our thoughts include worries, the result may be that we become anxious, experiencing fight-or-flight arousal without noticing why. This chapter will help you to pay more attention to your thoughts and specifically to become more aware of how much time you're spending engaged in worry. The other by-product of our incessant thinking is that we begin to experience our thoughts as the very center of who we are. We begin to believe "I am my thoughts." Steven Hayes and his colleagues have described this phenomenon as looking at the world *through* our thoughts rather than looking *at* our thoughts (1999). With help from the exercises in this chapter, you will begin to learn how to look at your thoughts.

MONITORING YOUR THOUGHTS

One of the easiest ways to become more aware of what you're thinking is to write down the thoughts that you are aware of. As you begin to monitor and record your thoughts, you will notice at first that it is difficult to put all that you are thinking into words. Your thoughts include not only words, but abstract ideas, fleeting memories, music, and images. Don't worry about faithfully recording everything that passes through your mind. Instead, try to capture the essence of what you're thinking in a phrase or sentence. Put the words in quotes to emphasize that these are "thoughts" produced by your mind. To get you started, try the following simple exercise.

EXERCISE 4.1: Watching Your Thoughts

You will need a pencil and paper. In this exercise, you will simply be observing your thoughts for a few moments and then writing down what you observed, describing your thoughts with a few phrases or sentences. You will be collecting two samples of your thoughts.

Sample A: In your head, slowly read the following list. As you read the list, observe your thoughts closely. When you are done, write down all of the thoughts that you were aware of having while you were reading the list. Put the thoughts in quotes, and label these thoughts "Sample A."

(Take a minute to "tune in" to your thoughts before you begin.)

chocolate	fudge swirl
butter pecan	strawberry
peppermint	pistachio
tutti-frutti	rocky road
banana	spumoni
thin mint	chocolate chip
vanilla	coffee

Sample B: Repeat the process you followed for Sample A with the following list. Record your thoughts in quotes, and label the resulting list of thoughts "Sample B."

orange	grape
cherry	mortgage
lemon	divorce
cancer	blood
taxes	retirement
sex	money
children	death

Were you able to capture some of your thoughts? Many people find this difficult to do the first time they try it. Monitoring and recording your thoughts will come more easily with practice. Look at the two samples of your thoughts. Are they similar? Notice how the content of your thoughts varies based on the triggers that you are responding to.

For Sample A, you were responding to a list with a very specific slant. It would be surprising if you did not think of ice cream at some point while reading this list. Other thoughts might have looked something like these:

"I hate coffee ice cream"

"Memory of going to the ice cream parlor with my dad"

"I eat too much ice cream"

"Mmmmmmmm ... c h o c o l a t e ..."

For Sample B, the trigger list included several items that might be more emotionally charged or loaded than the list of ice cream flavors. Notice that when emotions are activated, our thoughts may become more vivid or intense. On the one hand, this can make these thoughts easier to monitor. At other times, we might instinctively pull away from these thoughts or images and resist monitoring or recording them. As you begin to monitor and write down your thoughts, it will be important to remain open to observing even emotionally charged thoughts. Looking at these thoughts is the first step toward changing our relationship to them.

RECOGNIZING WORRY THOUGHTS

Many people who worry excessively report that they have done so from a very early age. If you have spent much of your life engaged in worry, it's likely that much of the time that you are worrying you don't even realize that you're doing so. As you begin to pay more attention to your thinking, you will notice that worry thoughts tend to follow certain patterns.

"What If ..." Thoughts

Perhaps the most classic type of worry is worry about the future and potential negative outcomes. This often takes the form of

"What if ..." thinking. Examples of this type of thinking would be thoughts like:

"What if I am in a fatal accident?"

"What if my house burns down while I'm out of town?"

"What if I develop cancer and die?"

At times, "What if ..." thinking can be useful. It can help us to prepare for certain likely outcomes. For example, if it is cloudy when you're leaving the house, the thought "What if it rains?" can prompt you to bring an umbrella. The "What if ..." thoughts that characterize worry, however, are about outcomes that we have little or no control over or that continue even after we have taken reasonable precautions. For example, if I have unplugged the iron and turned off the heater, how helpful is it for me to continue to have the thought "What if the house burns down while I'm away?"

One reason that worriers tend to do so much "What if ..." thinking has to do with their low tolerance for uncertainty. Often, they have a strong desire to know how things will turn out in the future. At times they may feel that they cannot make a decision until they know exactly what the outcome of that decision will be. Since the very nature of the future is that it is unknowable, it's impossible to ever truly know how any decision or action that you take will turn out. If you insist on having this knowledge before making a choice or taking action, you will become paralyzed. In an effort to reduce the uncertainty of the future, worriers generate "What if ..." thoughts. Since this process is rooted in anxiety to begin with, these thoughts tend to involve negative outcomes.

As you read in chapter 1, two things tend to happen when worriers think about negative outcomes: overestimation of probability and catastrophizing. When anticipating the ways in which things might go wrong, people who worry often overestimate the probability that things will turn out badly. They do this in spite of previous experience or other evidence that suggests that such an outcome is unlikely. For example, they might have the thought that they are likely to be mugged, even though they are walking in a neighborhood where muggings rarely occur. Or, they might worry that they will develop pneumonia when they have a minor cold. Alternatively, these worriers anticipate that when something bad happens, they will be unable to cope. Bad things inevitably happen to all of us. It is likely that you have already experienced a number of very difficult events in your life and managed them, though perhaps with some difficulty. When we catastrophize, we imagine that when bad things happen we will be unable to manage or respond to them.

EXERCISE 4.2:
Noticing "What if ..." Thoughts

Make a list of any "What if ..." thoughts that you can remember having in the past few days or weeks. Notice whether these thoughts involve overestimation of the probability of a negative outcome or catastrophizing.

Rumination

Sometimes worry takes the form of persistent thoughts and anxiety about things that happened in the past. Psychologists call this type of thinking *rumination*. When we are ruminating, we are thinking and worrying about events that have already taken place. Our thoughts about these events often have an analytic quality. We might think about something that someone said and ask ourselves, "What did he mean by that?" We might remember something that we did and anxiously think, "I wish I hadn't done that!" or "If only I could have said *that* instead!" Rumination is often accompanied by an intense wish to turn the clock back and to be able to redo a specific situation or event.

Another form that rumination can take is the "Why?" question. There is no answer to the "Why?" question, so asking it is often upsetting and usually counterproductive. Here are some examples:

"Why can't I make as much money as Bill Gates?"

"Why is my boss so critical and hard to please?"

"Why can't everyone follow the rules of the road?"

"Why did it have to rain today, of all days?"

"Why me?"

What is implied by the "Why?" questions is that things shouldn't be the way they are. By asking the "Why?" question, we are rejecting what is, and ruling it out of order. Doing this is like having an allergic reaction to reality, making it more difficult for us to respond effectively.

Rumination is nonproductive by definition. Rather than helping us to function better, it tends to produce feelings of anxiety, guilt, or depression. Thinking about negative events in the past is only helpful when we are faced with a choice in the present that we have made before. At these times, it may be useful to remember earlier choices and outcomes, but only briefly. Sometimes, a thought that is helpful at one point in time is nonproductive rumination at another. For example, suppose you had the following thought about the clothes you decided to wear to work on Monday morning:

"Did I wear this exact same outfit to work on Friday?"

If you have this thought in the morning, before you leave the house, it might be a useful thought. If you discover that you did indeed wear those exact clothes the last time you went to work, you have the opportunity to change into something different. However, suppose you are having this thought after you have already arrived at work. At this point, the thought is nonproductive, and could be classified as rumination.

Rumination on the past tends to produce not only anxiety but often feelings of guilt and depression as well. Guilt can be described as a very specific form of anxiety that is focused on events that have happened in the past. Like all anxiety, guilt can serve a useful function in our lives. Feelings of guilt alert us to choices that violate our personal ethical and moral code of conduct. When guilt persists even after it has served the purpose of warning us away from making or repeating a certain choice, it is rumination and is likely to be counterproductive.

Whenever rumination about past choices or past events is accompanied by a strong wish to reverse or change those choices or events, we are likely to develop feelings of depression. Depression, characterized by shutting down and making limited responses to the environment, often results when people are in situations in which they are helpless and do not have or perceive options for responding.

Since we have no direct access to the past and can't change past events, rumination places us in just such a situation of helplessness. Directing our energy and desire for control toward events in the past is like trying to move a mountain by pushing on it. Like the mountain, the past is fixed and unmovable. The harder we push against this fixed reality, the more discomfort we are likely to experience.

EXERCISE 4.3: Noticing Rumination

Make a list of any ruminations about the past that you can remember having in the past few days or weeks. Notice whether these thoughts were related to feelings of anxiety, guilt, or depression.

WORRY VS. PLANNING & PROBLEM SOLVING

In the first chapter, we saw that one reason people continue to worry is that while they are engaged in the process of worrying, they actually believe that they are planning or problem solving. Believing that they are doing something useful and productive, worriers are anxious about letting go of worrisome thoughts. "If I stop worrying, my problems will get the best of me" is a common thought. Remember that worry is nonproductive by definition. Understanding the difference between planning or problem solving and worry will help you to recognize when you are engaged in nonproductive thinking and label those thoughts as worry.

Planning

One of the most important abilities of human beings is our ability to imagine and predict future events. Like language and thinking, this ability sets us apart as a species. Planning has allowed us to master our environment in many ways, both for better and for worse. Verbally describing our future actions step-by-step is essential to every man-made accomplishment from a ham sandwich to a skyscraper. When we are planning, we are simply making a sequential list of actions we intend to take. Imagining future events in this way allows us to determine the best way to sequence those actions and to anticipate problems that might arise. These actions might include reasonable precautions to prevent or avoid anticipated problems. When we imagine future events or problems when there are no actions or precautions that we can take, we are no longer planning—we are worrying.

Problem Solving

It is often through the process of planning that we first become aware of problems. Other times, problems present themselves unexpectedly. Our first reaction to problems always involves a certain degree of anxiety. Remember that this anxiety or fight-or-flight arousal is our natural, biologically programmed response to a perceived threat. A problem is one type of perceived threat. When presented with an immediate or an anticipated problem, it helps if we can engage in an effective process of problem solving. We are problem solving when we are generating possible solutions and evaluating them. Through this process, we are able to choose a course of action to take. When we think about a problem without generating possible solutions or evaluating them, we are not problem solving, we are worrying.

To determine whether you are engaged in planning or problem solving versus worrying, consider the outcome of the process:

Process	Outcome
Planning	List of actions and reasonable precautions
Problem solving	Generation and evaluation of possible solutions
Worrying	Increased anxiety, procrastination, and avoidance

When we are at our most productive, it is common to go back and forth between the two processes of planning and problem solving. In the course of planning, we encounter an anticipated problem and switch to problem-solving mode. We list solutions, pick the best one, and return to planning mode to plan the implementation of that solution. In a later chapter, we will review the components of effective planning and problem solving in more detail.

NOTICING YOUR WORRY TRIGGERS

Paying attention to the people, places, and events that tend to trigger worry will help you to recognize worry more readily. The purpose of identifying worry triggers is not so that you can avoid them. Instead, being aware of common worry triggers can help you to more readily identify situations in which you are likely to react with the control response described earlier. This increased awareness can make it easier to apply the LLAMP approach. Rather than avoiding these worry triggers, it often makes more sense to seek them out. In chapter 9, we will explore how avoiding these situations can actually intensify their ability to trigger worry and anxiety over time.

Worry triggers can include situations like traveling, social interactions, being sick, or having an important responsibility. Specific people can also be triggers for worry. For example, many people worry excessively about family members and loved ones or find that their own worries are triggered when they are around people who express a great deal of worry. There may be certain places where you are more likely to worry, for example work or public places may trigger more worry than home. For people who toss and turn at night, bed can actually become a trigger for worry. Finally, worry can be triggered by any number of behaviors or activities. For example, balancing your checkbook, trying on new clothes, or even watching the nightly news can all be triggers for worry.

EXERCISE 4.4:
Be Aware of Worry Triggers

Make a list of your worry triggers. Try to identify situations, people, places, and behaviors that trigger worry. Be on the lookout for worry when these triggers come up. Rather than avoiding these triggers, try to see them as an opportunity to practice the LLAMP approach.

IDENTIFY YOUR WORRY THEMES

What are the things that you worry about? Most worriers find that their worries can be separated into a number of themes. For example: worries about health, worries about relationships, worries about finances, worries about catastrophic events. Within each of these worry themes, people experience specific worry thoughts. For example, the theme "worries about health" might include thoughts like "What if I develop cancer?" or "My heart is racing. Could something be wrong?"

Making a list of your worry themes will be helpful in noticing and labeling worry when it occurs. It will also be useful when you begin the structured exposure exercises described in chapter 9.

EXERCISE 4.5:
Identify your Worry Themes

List your most common worry themes. Under each, list two or three examples of specific worry thoughts that you typically have about each theme. Look at the worries that you came up with in the previous exercises to make a list that is as complete as possible.

Example:

Theme: Worries about my job

"My boss doesn't talk to me much. Does he dislike me?"

"What if I don't get this project completed on time?"

"If I lost my job, could I find another one?"

Theme: Worries about my marriage

"My wife seems preoccupied. Is she angry with me?"

"Should I call her at work to check in?"

"What will I do if my marriage falls apart?"

Theme: Financial worries

"What if I don't have enough money in my checking account?"

"Why can't I make as much money as my brother-in-law?"

"Why did I buy that expensive dinner last night?"

NOTICE WORRY-RELATED FEELINGS

There may be a wide range of feelings that you associate with worry. Perhaps you feel jumpy and restless. Other people describe feeling uncomfortable in their own skin. Worry is sometimes accompanied by feelings of frustration, irritability, and annoyance. Perhaps the most frightening and uncomfortable feeling for some worriers is a sense of impending doom. People who experience this feeling will often say things like "I just know something terrible is going to happen." Psychologists call this type of thinking *hypervigilance*. Part of the fight-or-flight response, hypervigilance involves the brain processing information in a biased way, scanning the environment specifically looking for a threat. When this response is fully aroused, we are likely to find threats at every turn, whether they are real or imagined. If we were living in the forest, we would have the sense that predators were lurking behind every tree or rock and we would startle at any movement or sound. The thoughts of impending doom that accompany hypervigilance are irrational but difficult to disprove. The fact is that *something* bad will happen to everyone eventually. If we live long enough, each one of us will get critically ill, have a serious accident, or lose loved ones. These events are part of life and will happen at some point whether we anticipate and dread them or not. The problem is, we have no idea of when these things will happen and, specifically, which events lie in store for us. What we do know is that the struggle with feelings of impending doom not only fails to protect us from the future but interferes with our ability to get the most out of the present.

Whether worry for you tends to be associated with feelings of doom and dread, restlessness, irritability, or discomfort, notice these feelings when they occur. Remember that these feelings are part of your experience "inside" and that your goal is therefore not to control or get rid of them but to observe and to experience them. Feelings are to be felt. That is all that we can do with them. *Feel* your feelings, making room for them as part of your experience. Also, pay attention to the thoughts that accompany these feelings.

EXERCISE 4.6: Describe Your Feelings

Try to describe the feelings you experience when you worry. Make a list of these feelings. Assigning words to your feelings (labeling them) can make it easier to notice and observe them.

NOTICE BODY SENSATIONS

In chapter 1 you were introduced to the fight-or-flight response that is part of all anxiety and worry. This increased arousal is experienced as a number of bodily sensations. Each individual is likely to be more aware of or more bothered by certain sensations than by others. Some of the sensations that people associate with worry include pounding or racing heartbeat, muscle pain and tension, muscle twitching or jumping, trembling or shaking, jaw clenching, tingling sensations on the skin, cold hands and feet, shortness of breath, dizziness or light-headedness, hot flashes, blurred vision, sweating, butterflies in the stomach, nausea, and dry mouth. Look back at the description of the fight-or-flight response in chapter 1 for an explanation of the bodily changes that cause all of these sensations and how they helped us to survive when we were living in forested areas surrounded by predators.

Today these physical changes are mostly unnecessary—but also completely unavoidable. Body sensations fall into the inside category of experience along with thoughts and feelings. The harder we try to stop or get rid of these sensations, the more we seem to have them. Noticing and labeling them will make it easier to begin to make room for them as part of your experience.

EXERCISE 4.7:
Notice Your Body Sensations

Select one of the worry themes that has been most upsetting to you lately. Close your eyes for a few minutes and think about this theme. Allow yourself to engage in some "What if ..." thinking and to imagine the worst-case scenario. Notice how your body reacts to these thoughts and images. In your mind, take a scan of your body from your toes, up your legs, across your torso, down your arms, across your back and shoulders, up your neck, and into your head. Notice all of the sensations that you're aware of. Make a list of all the body sensations you felt and any other sensations that you have associated with worry in the past. Assigning labels like "tingling," "tension," or "butterflies" to each sensation will make it easier to observe and eventually to accept these sensations when they are present.

IDENTIFY WORRY BEHAVIOR

"Worry behavior" is anything that you do in response to worry. Usually the behavior is directed at escaping or trying to get rid of anxiety and worry.

Avoidance

Perhaps the most common type of worry behavior is avoidance. This can take many forms. You might choose to avoid certain situations, places, or activities that are triggers for worry. For example, if you tend to worry about illness or dying you may avoid visiting a hospital or reading the obituaries. If you are worried about being the victim of a crime, you might avoid watching certain news reports. Perhaps you respond to your worries about finances by putting off balancing your checkbook. Worriers also avoid taking on new projects or pursuing their dreams because they fear failing. By not taking that promotion or that sculpting class, they are able to avoid the anxiety that comes with trying something new and worries about not being good enough. Most worry behaviors are avoidance of one type or another. What are you avoiding in these instances? Usually it is the thoughts, feelings, and sensations that constitute inside experience. These are the "passengers on the bus." Unfortunately, as you recall, avoiding these passengers involves taking constant detours and carries the heavy cost of living a life other than the one you truly want to live.

Procrastination

When we procrastinate, we are engaged in a type of avoidance that we tell ourselves is only temporary but that is often part of a bigger pattern that keeps us from moving toward the things we value most. Procrastination is often a way to avoid thinking about certain things and experiencing the anxiety related to those thoughts. Many people who procrastinate are perfectionistic and set unrealistic standards for themselves surrounding a specific task. This produces anxiety around the task, which they then avoid by putting it off. At its most extreme, procrastination can take the form of freezing up, spacing out, or becoming "paralyzed." People who experience this phenomenon experience a sense of threat so vague that any response seems to be the wrong one. Like a deer in the headlights, they temporarily shut down. The problem with procrastination, aside from the obvious one of a failure to move forward in life, is that the very act of procrastination usually makes the avoided task even more anxiety provoking than it was before. This can then lead to more procrastination in a viciously escalating cycle.

Interpersonal Avoidance

Many people who have trouble with worry avoid a variety of social situations, particularly those that call for assertiveness. Worriers may avoid events where they are likely to meet new people or run into someone that they are having a conflict with. When running into people they know, they may avoid getting into conversations or making eye contact. They may shy away from speaking up in groups or expressing their opinions because of worries about what others will think. *Assertiveness* involves asking for what we need and saying no to others. These are two things that many worriers avoid doing. As a result, many of them often feel overcommitted and that they are spending more time doing what others want them to do than doing what they believe to be important. Failure to speak up, ask for what you need or want, or to say no to a request are all forms of avoidance.

Reassurance Seeking or Checking

Other worry behaviors that provide us with a temporary escape from uncomfortable feelings involve seeking out reassurance of one form or another. This is really just another form of avoidance, in that the reassurance helps us to temporarily avoid thoughts and feelings that will be there waiting for us once the initial wave of reassurance subsides. Examples of reassurance seeking include making frequent phone calls to loved ones to make sure they are safe, checking and double-checking things to make sure they were done or done correctly, and excessive apologizing or checking in with others to make sure that we have not offended them.

Worriers often have trouble telling the difference between taking reasonable precautions and worry behavior. How much checking is too much checking? To figure this out, it's necessary to appeal to the most rational part of your mind. There are times when checking may serve a concrete purpose and times when its only purpose is to immediately reduce anxiety. When there is a concrete function to checking, it is usually served by checking something *once*. After that, most checking is worry behavior. A useful rule of thumb is the "mailbox rule." After dropping a letter into a public mailbox, it may be useful to pull the door open once to make sure that the letter dropped down into the box. This is a reasonable precaution. Checking a second time implies the suspicion that the letter has jumped out of the box and is somehow resisting being mailed. Since this is not rational, checking twice equals worry behavior.

Superstitious Behavior

To some extent, certain superstitious beliefs are part of every culture. People who engage in excessive worry, however, often pay more attention to superstitions and develop their own individualized superstitious beliefs and behaviors. This might take the form of avoiding certain activities at certain times or engaging in specific behaviors or rituals to correct or prevent negative outcomes. For example, people who are looking forward to a specific event may be afraid to talk about it for fear that they will "jinx" the outcome. Other superstitious behaviors include rituals completed before leaving the house to assure a safe return, sitting in a specific part of a bus or airplane, or carrying a certain item around based on the belief that "you never need it until you don't have it." The problem with superstitious behaviors is that they are self-reinforcing. When the expected tragedy fails to occur, the belief in the power of the superstitious behavior is strengthened.

Compulsive Behaviors

For many people, worry and anxiety are accompanied by a variety of nervous habits like nail-biting, foot-tapping, finger-drumming, playing with or pulling hair, knuckle-cracking, and even rocking. These are purposeless expressions of fight-or-flight arousal, but in their most extreme form can be harmful to the worrier and disruptive to others. Other compulsive responses to worry include overeating, not eating, and alcohol and drug use. All of these behaviors are subtle to not-so-subtle forms of emotional and experiential avoidance. Becoming more aware of these behaviors will help you to be more aware of worry. Blocking or preventing these behaviors will provide you with the opportunity to observe, experience, and eventually accept the thoughts, feelings, and sensations that the compulsive behaviors help you to temporarily avoid or diminish.

EXERCISE 4.8:
Notice Your Worry Behaviors

Make a list of your most common worry behaviors. Think about situations, people, and places that you might avoid. List any tasks that you respond to with procrastination. Are there any interpersonal situations that you avoid? Times you avoid being assertive? List any checking or reassurance-seeking behaviors as well as anything you do that is guided by a superstitious belief. Finally, do you have any compulsive habits that are associated with worry?

MONITORING WORRY

Now that you have taken the time to think about and identify your most common worry triggers as well as the different types of thoughts, feelings, and bodily sensations that you associate with worry and how you respond to these behaviorally, it is time to apply this awareness by monitoring your worry throughout the day. While you may feel that you already spend enough time thinking about worry, it's likely that much of this time is spent struggling to push worry away and to avoid the anxiety that accompanies it. As we discussed in the last two chapters, this strategy has not been very effective. By beginning to actively watch for worry and labeling it as "worry" when it starts, you are actually less likely to become swept up into your usual, automatic engagement with the worry thoughts and your struggling resistance to anxious feelings.

Outside/Inside Monitoring

Use the monitoring format pictured in figure 4.1 to record worry when it occurs over the next several days. You can make copies of this page and carry them with you or log worry in your notebook using this outside/inside format. Try to carry a monitoring form with you at all times. When you become aware of anxiety or worry, try to record all components of your worry experience right away. It may be tempting to wait until the end of the day and then to try to reconstruct the worry, but this is much less effective. Not only will you not remember all of the details of your worrying experience, but the act of recording worry in-the-moment will help you begin to develop more objectivity and distance from your thoughts, feelings, and sensations.

On the left-hand side of the monitoring form, record the situation, person, or event that triggered the worry. If you are not sure what the trigger was, just write down where you were and what time of day the worrying started. Next, inside the box, write down any worry-related thoughts, feelings, or sensations that you are aware of. Put the thoughts in quotes to remind yourself that these are only thoughts. On the right-hand side of the page, outside of the box, record any worry behaviors that you notice. If you noticed any checking or other types of avoidance, for example, record that here. Look at the sample monitoring form in figure 4.2.

NOTICE & LABEL WORRY THOUGHTS

By monitoring your worry in a focused and structured way for several days, you will begin to develop a more objective perspective from which to consider your thoughts, feelings, and sensations. You will begin to look *at* your thoughts rather than seeing the world *through* your thoughts, which will eventually allow you to respond to them in a different way. Recording your thoughts will also help you to be aware of the outside/inside distinction. As you learn and practice all of the LLAMP steps, you will apply the first four (LLAM) to everything that you are recording inside the box on the monitoring form. You will apply the last step (P) to everything outside the box.

Noticing and labeling your worry thoughts is the first step in the LLAMP approach. Often, when you apply this step, your fight-or-flight response will have already been activated. The next chapter will help you to let go of the impulse toward control that often accompanies this response, making room for the steps that follow.

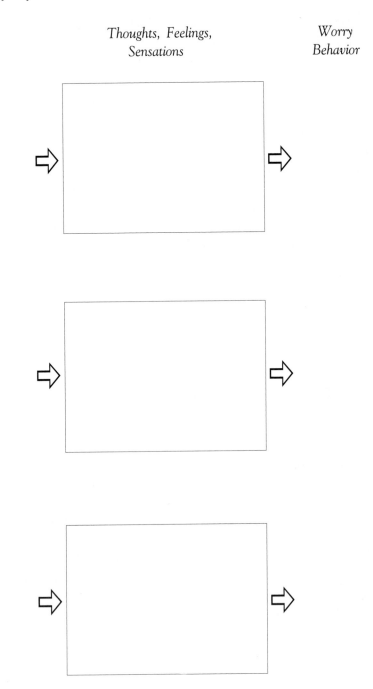

Figure 4.1: OUTSIDE/INSIDE MONITORING

| Worry
Triggers | Thoughts, Feelings,
Sensations | Worry
Behavior |

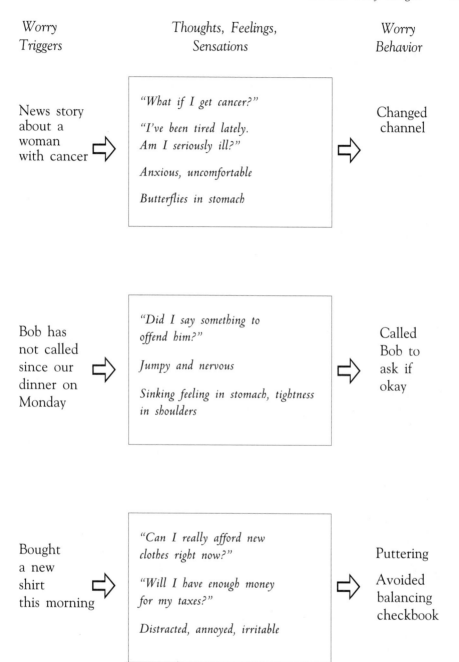

Worry Triggers	Thoughts, Feelings, Sensations	Worry Behavior
News story about a woman with cancer ⇒	*"What if I get cancer?"* *"I've been tired lately. Am I seriously ill?"* *Anxious, uncomfortable* *Butterflies in stomach*	⇒ Changed channel
Bob has not called since our dinner on Monday ⇒	*"Did I say something to offend him?"* *Jumpy and nervous* *Sinking feeling in stomach, tightness in shoulders*	⇒ Called Bob to ask if okay
Bought a new shirt this morning ⇒	*"Can I really afford new clothes right now?"* *"Will I have enough money for my taxes?"* *Distracted, annoyed, irritable*	⇒ Puttering Avoided balancing checkbook

Figure 4.2: OUTSIDE/INSIDE MONITORING

CHAPTER FIVE

LET GO OF CONTROL

Fight-or-flight arousal is a central part of the experience of worry. As you recall from chapter 1, the primary function of fight-or-flight arousal is to prepare you to take control of some aspect of your environment in order to get rid of the threat that triggered the response. In this way, fight-or-flight arousal is closely associated with the control instinct described in chapter 2. The focus of this chapter is to help you develop the ability to momentarily interrupt or slow down the fight-or-flight response and the automatic impulse to control or get rid of anxiety and worry that accompanies it. Many of the exercises presented could be described as relaxation exercises in that they often reduce anxiety and tension and produce feelings of relaxation and well-being.

As you practice these exercises, you will likely enjoy these feelings and hopefully experience a degree of relief from the muscle pain, headaches, and other problems associated with chronic overarousal. When you use these exercises in the context of the LLAMP approach, however, the goal is not to get rid of anxiety. Rather, the exercises, or sometimes small parts of the exercises, are used to temporarily and partially interrupt or interfere with the automatic response of control, making room for the new responses of acceptance and mindfulness described in the next two chapters.

ACCESSING THE
FIGHT-OR-FLIGHT RESPONSE

If you consider the list of physical changes that are part of the fight-or-flight response, you'll notice that most of these are changes in physical functions that you do not have direct access to. Changes like an increase in heart rate, changes in blood flow and in digestion, widening of the pupils, and perspiration are difficult if not impossible to consciously control. There are two physical processes involved in fight-or-flight arousal, however, that you do have varying degrees of access to: breathing and muscle tension. Of the two, you are most easily able to manipulate your breathing. You can change the rate at which you breathe, whether you breathe shallowly or deeply, and whether you breathe through your mouth or through your nose. By manipulating how you breathe, it's possible to slow down and even reverse the fight-or-flight response. To a lesser degree, you also have control over the level of tension in your muscles. For example, by making a fist, it is easy for most people to make the muscles in their arms tighter. What is more difficult but not impossible is to make your muscles more relaxed.

Through practicing the exercises presented here it is possible to learn how to relax not only the muscles in your arms, but muscles in your shoulders, back, jaw, face, and other areas where chronic tension is a problem. When using the LLAMP approach, it is not necessary to relax any particular group of muscles or for your muscles to remain relaxed. Rather, temporarily relaxing *some* of your muscles can serve as a symbolic reminder to let go of control in preparation for accepting and being mindful of your thoughts, feelings, and sensations. Paradoxically, the sensations you are preparing to accept by letting go of control may even include muscle tension.

Before we look at specific ways to change your breathing and relax your muscles, it is important to understand one other aspect of how the fight-or-flight response operates. In some ways, the fight-or-flight response is an all-or-nothing deal. All of the changes associated with fight-or-flight arousal are controlled by a special part of your nervous system called the *sympathetic nervous system*. Once a threat has passed and your body begins to relax, another response, opposite to the fight-or-flight response, kicks in. This is called the *relaxation response*, and it is governed by a completely separate system called the *parasympathetic nervous system*. The important thing to understand about these two systems is that they cannot operate simultaneously. They are like two elevator operators, one that only knows how to go up, and one that only knows how to go down. Your body is the elevator, and only one operator is working at any given time.

BREATHING

Before we discuss breathing in detail, take a few minutes to perform this simple test.

EXERCISE 5.1: The Breathing Test

Sit up straight in a comfortable chair with your feet flat on the floor. Put one hand flat on your chest, and put your other hand flat on your stomach, right over your belly button. Take several slow, deep breaths. Notice which of your hands is moving. Which hand moves the most as you breathe in? Do you breathe primarily in your chest or mostly in your belly? If you breathe both in your chest and in your belly, where is the breathing initiated? What percentage of the movement is in your chest versus in your belly? Is it fifty/fifty? Eighty/twenty?

Generally speaking, there are two ways that you can breathe: high in your chest, or low in your abdomen. Along with how fast you breathe, where you are breathing (chest or abdomen) at any given time will have a significant impact on how you are feeling. Breathing slowly, low down in the abdomen, is associated with feelings of calm and relaxation. Abdominal or "belly breathing" results in an increased supply of oxygen to your muscles, promoting relaxation. It also stimulates the relaxation response of the parasympathetic nervous system.

For most of us, when we are relaxed and resting, our breathing occurs primarily in the belly. When we are engaged in belly breathing, we are using a muscle called the *diaphragm*, which is just beneath the rib cage. If you have ever watched babies sleeping, you will notice that they breathe almost exclusively with their bellies. When we encounter a threatening or stressful situation and the fight-or-flight response kicks in, even slightly, most people begin to breathe higher in the chest. Some people have developed the habit of breathing high in their chest most of the time, even when they are not particularly stressed or anxious.

Chest breathing produces a series of changes in the normal operation of your body. First, breathing high in your chest reduces the level of carbon dioxide in your body, lowering the acid content of your blood. The body reacts to this low acid or *alkaline blood* by narrowing the blood vessels in certain parts of the body. The result is a restriction in blood flow to the brain and certain other tissues. This change is not dangerous; however, it is part of the fight-or-flight response and triggers all of the other physical changes associated with fight-or-flight arousal. The effects of chest breathing can be subtle at times. Even slight chest breathing, continuing over a long period of time, can set you up for an acute fight-or-flight reaction in response to even mild stressors.

Learning to breathe primarily in your belly, using your diaphragm, can reduce your baseline level of anxiety and arousal throughout the day. When you are confronted with a sudden increase in worry or anxiety, taking a few deep belly breaths can help you to let go of the control impulse and better apply the acceptance and mindfulness strategies discussed in the next two chapters. If you have been primarily a chest breather for a long time, beginning to breathe from your belly may be a bit difficult or uncomfortable at first. Regular use of the following exercise will make it easier over time by stretching your diaphragm and helping you to identify what proper belly breathing feels like.

EXERCISE 5.2: The Phone Book Exercise

You will need a large phone book for this exercise. Lie flat on your back on the floor. You may stretch out your legs or bend your knees for more comfort. Rest the phone book on your belly. The book should lie just below your rib cage and cover your belly button. Let your arms rest at your sides. Breathing in through your nose, try to pull your breath all the way down to your navel. The first goal of this exercise is to move the phone book as high as possible with each intake of breath. This should be accomplished strictly by breathing.

You might imagine that you are inflating a balloon inside your stomach, which then raises the phone book. At the top of the inhale, pause for a second or two, then slowly exhale through your mouth.

Exhale slowly and completely. Pause again, then take another breath in, remembering to breathe through your nose. Feel the phone book moving up and down with each breath in and out. The second goal of the exercise is to relax your body. As you continue to breathe slowly and deeply, allow your shoulders and arms to relax, sinking into the floor. Allow your back and your head to be fully supported by the floor. Imagine all of your muscles relaxing.

    This exercise stretches and strengthens the diaphragm and other muscles involved in proper belly breathing. By focusing on what it feels like to breathe in this way, you will become more familiar with how to use your diaphragm and will most likely find it easier to breathe from your belly at other times, even in a sitting or standing position. At first, practicing while lying on your back in this way may be easier than belly breathing while seated or standing, since when you are lying on your back there is less weight on top of your diaphragm. The reason the instructions specify breathing in through your nose and out through your mouth has to do with the rate of air flow. Often when we have trouble getting a full, deep breath, it is because we have failed to exhale completely. When there is old air trapped in the lungs, there is not as much room for new air. Since the mouth is larger than the nose (for most people), you will get more air out faster by exhaling through your mouth. Breathing in through your nose assures that you are not taking air in too quickly, which can lead to some of the same problems associated with chest breathing.

    Start by practicing the Phone Book Exercise at least once every day for ten or fifteen minutes. A good time to practice is at the end of the day, before getting into bed. It is best to practice on the floor rather than in bed so that you don't fall asleep before completing the exercise. Try to make this breathing practice part of your routine, like brushing your teeth. If you like, you can put a note on your toothbrush as a reminder.

Remembering to Breathe

    Once you get a feel for belly breathing while lying on your back, begin to practice it while sitting up or standing throughout the day. Try to associate breathing practice with any moments of downtime that come up on a daily basis. For example, when you are driving, the time spent waiting at traffic signals is an ideal time to practice belly breathing. Waiting for your computer to start up when you first turn it on or waiting for a document to print are also good times to take a few slow, deep abdominal breaths. Try letting the telephone ring one extra ring, allowing just enough time for one belly breath before answering. Other places and times to practice belly breathing include standing in line at the supermarket, waiting for the microwave to heat a snack, waiting for the elevator, riding in the elevator, waiting for a bus or the subway, watching television, listening to music, standing in the shower, while washing dishes, and right now, while reading this book. By remembering to take slow, deep belly breaths throughout the day, you will eventually begin to breathe with your belly most of the time without even thinking about it. In addition, building deep, mindful breaths into your daily routine is a great way to put more "spaces" into your day, slowing down the pace a bit. You will most likely find that slowing the pace in this way does not mean being less productive. In fact, the opposite is often true.

EXERCISE 5.3: Remembering to Breathe

At a stationery store, get about a dozen small decorative stickers that you like. Put the stickers in different places where you are likely to see them throughout the day: in your car, on the refrigerator, on your key ring, on the bathroom mirror, on your desk, on the hairdryer, etc. As you go through your day, whenever you see one of these stickers, take a slow, deep abdominal breath. Pause, then let it out slowly.

Breathing to Let Go of Control

The way you breathe throughout the day has a lot to do with your body's *baseline arousal*. This is the level of arousal you experience most of the day while sitting or moving about at a regular speed. It's the body's equivalent of a car's idle speed. If you tend to chest breathe most of the time, you may be someone with a "high idle," also known as a type A personality. Type A's tend to have higher blood pressure and are more likely to develop stress-related illnesses. They are also more prone to worry. As you practice belly breathing and become more comfortable using your diaphragm to breathe throughout the day, you may experience a lower level of baseline arousal. If you are starting from a more relaxed baseline, you may not be as quick to reach such high levels of anxiety even when you do find that you are worrying. You might also find that belly breathing offers some relief from muscle aches and pains by reducing your level of muscle tension throughout the day. Belly breathing is associated with more relaxed muscles since it allows more oxygen to reach the muscle tissues.

While reducing your baseline anxiety and muscle tension is great, when you use belly breathing in the context of the LLAMP approach, you will do so with a different end in mind. In those moments when you are faced with increasing anxiety and worry, trying to "breathe away" your feelings is not likely to work, and it may even lead to more frustration and increased discomfort. Instead, use belly breathing in conjunction with relaxing your muscles slightly as a way to remember to let go of control. Belly breathing will help you to relax your muscles, and this can help you to avoid "bearing down" on your anxious feelings and worry thoughts. Remember, tense muscles and other elements of fight-or-flight arousal are part of the control response. Relaxing your muscles will help you to let go of this response.

MUSCLE TENSION

Perhaps the most remarkable physical change that occurs during the fight-or-flight response is the increased muscle tension experienced in the large muscles of the arms, legs, back, shoulders, neck, and jaw. This makes sense, because we use these muscles for both fighting and "flighting." Increased tension in the muscles of the shoulders, back, and arms prepare us to take on our enemies in hand-to-hand combat. It can also leave us with a sore back and result in shaking and trembling of the arms and hands. The clenching and grinding of the jaw muscles is a similarly aggressive response that leaves the muscles of the face and head tight and can result in face pain, headaches, and ringing of the ears. Tension in the large muscles of the legs prepares us to run from predators and can also contribute to pain and muscle cramps.

When you do the exercises that follow, it will help if you keep in mind what muscle tension is. On a mechanical level, muscles become tense because they are filled with blood. When blood is trapped in the muscle for a long period of time, toxins begin to build up in the muscle tissue. In the tense-and-release exercises that follow, you will learn to mechanically pump blood and toxins out of your muscles by tightening and releasing them. This allows a fresh supply of blood to enter the muscle, which you will experience as a warming or relaxing sensation. Deep abdominal breathing facilitates this relaxation of the muscles by increasing the level of oxygen in the tissues.

In all of the exercises that follow, you will breathe in while tensing your muscles and breathe out when relaxing them. Exhaling and relaxing your muscles will eventually become triggers for letting go of the control response. When tensing each muscle group, be sure to tighten the muscles vigorously, but be careful not to overdo it. It is not necessary to strain or to tighten them as tightly as possible. As you exhale and slowly release, focus on the sensations associated with relaxing the muscle and think the words "let go" to yourself. First practice each step of these exercises with your eyes open, reading each step as you go. Once you have learned all of the steps, do the exercise all the way through slowly, with your eyes closed. If you like, you can make an audiotape of yourself reading the instructions slowly out loud, then listen to the tape as you do the exercise.

EXERCISE 5.4:
Extended Muscle Relaxation

Sit up straight in a comfortable chair that has good back support. Rest both feet flat on the floor. Close your eyes. Take a deep breath and release it slowly. On the next inhale:

1. Curl your toes tightly. Pause for a moment, then as you exhale, release and relax your toes, thinking "let go ..." Focus on how it feels to relax your toes. Notice the difference between how your feet feel when your toes are tensed and how they feel when you relax. Repeat this step.

2. Lifting the balls of your feet off the floor, point your toes toward the ceiling, flexing your feet upward. Inhale deeply, then pause. Allowing your toes to slowly return to the floor, exhale slowly, focusing on the muscles in the front of your lower legs. Notice how they feel as they become more relaxed. Think "let go ..."

3. Now raise your heels toward the ceiling, keeping your toes on the floor. Notice the muscles in the back of your lower legs as they tighten. Inhale deeply, then pause a moment. On the exhale, slowly relax, focusing on how it feels for the muscles to release.

4. Breathing in, move your knees toward one another. As you press your knees inward (they need not touch), notice the muscles on the insides of your thighs getting tighter. As you exhale, relax these muscles, allowing your knees to fall apart.

5. Now move your knees apart, tightening the muscles on the outsides of your thighs, as well as your buttocks. Inhale slowly. As you exhale and think "let go," allow your knees to come closer together, relaxing all of your muscles.

6. Sitting up straighter in the chair, thrust your chest forward slightly and raise your shoulders toward your ears. Take a deep breath as you hold your torso erect. Pause for a moment. As you exhale slowly, relax your back and let your shoulders drop, allowing yourself to sink into the back of the chair. Notice how your back and shoulder muscles feel as they relax.

7. Inhaling, open your mouth and raise your eyebrows, making the features of your face as big as possible. Holding your breath, purse your lips and squint your eyes, making your face as small as possible. As you exhale, relax your face completely, allowing your jaw to drop.

8. Make fists with both hands and bend your arms at the elbow, bringing your fists toward your shoulders. Hold your fists and arms tight as you inhale. Pause. Exhaling, slowly lower your arms and release your fists. Noticing how the muscles of your arms feel as they relax, say to yourself "let go ..."

Continue to breathe slowly and deeply, allowing all of your muscles to become more relaxed with each breath. If you are aware of any tension in your body, imagine breathing air into that part of your body. Then imagine the tension draining away as you exhale, again saying to yourself "let go." Enjoy this relaxed state as long as you like before opening your eyes.

As you do this exercise, it is important to focus on how your muscles feel when they are tense and how they feel as they relax. By attending to this very closely, you are teaching yourself to discriminate between tension and relaxation in your muscles. Often, you may not even realize that muscle groups are tight until you begin to tense and relax them. By training yourself to feel muscles relax, you will eventually be able to relax muscles just by concentrating on relaxing them, without having to tense them first. Once again, breathing deeply will help with this. Remember to breathe in through your nose and out through your mouth and to use your diaphragm. Concentrate on relaxing your muscles as you exhale. In the beginning, it will be helpful to practice this exercise in its entirety once or twice every day. It should take about fifteen minutes if you take your time and really focus on the sensations as you relax. Try doing this exercise once or twice every day for a full week before moving on to the next exercise.

While taking the time to relax all of your muscle groups is a good strategy to start with, it is helpful to eventually learn to relax more quickly. After you have mastered exercise 5.4 and are able to relax all of your muscle groups, move on to the following exercise. This three-step exercise can be completed in less than sixty seconds and can therefore be used several times throughout the day.

EXERCISE 5.5:
Abbreviated Muscle Relaxation

Sitting up straight with your back supported by the chair and your feet on the floor, begin by taking a deep breath in, holding it for a moment, then releasing it slowly. On the next inhale:

1. Raise your toes toward the ceiling and bring your knees together, tightening the muscles in the front of your legs and inside your thighs. Hold the breath for a moment, then slowly exhale, relaxing your muscles as you do so, allowing your knees to fall apart and your toes to return to the floor. Think "let go ..."

2. Breathing in, raise your heels off the floor, moving your knees apart, tensing the muscles at the back of your legs and in your buttocks. Pause, then slowly exhale, thinking "let go ..." and relaxing the muscles in your legs.

3. Breathing in, tighten both hands into fists at your sides. Bending your elbows, bring your fists up to your shoulders. Shrugging your shoulders, raise them toward your ears. Hold the breath at the top of your inhale. As you exhale slowly, gradually lower your shoulders and open your fists. As you do this, think to yourself: "let go ..."

This exercise can be repeated throughout the day. Try to incorporate this "sixty-second break" into all of those moments of downtime mentioned above in the section on belly breathing. Use the stickers from exercise 5.3 as reminders to relax your muscles in this way throughout the day.

Eventually, you will be able to achieve a more relaxed state without tensing your muscles at all. After you have experienced some success with the tense-and-relax exercises, try to notice when your muscles are getting tense and to relax them simply by taking a deep breath and reminding yourself to let go.

EXERCISE 5.6: Relaxing On Cue

1. Notice the parts of your body where you are most aware of tension.

2. Take a deep belly breath, imagining the breath moving into the tense parts of your body.

3. Pause for a moment.

4. Exhale slowly, relaxing and releasing the tension. Think "let go ..."

5. Repeat as needed.

LETTING GO OF CONTROL

As you develop this letting-go response and begin to use it in the context of the LLAMP approach to worry and anxiety, it is important to have an idea of what it is that you're letting go of. As applied in the LLAMP approach, letting go does not mean letting go of anxiety or worry. Rather, it means letting go of attempts to *control* anxiety and worry. It's about letting go of the struggle with anxiety and worry.

The Monster and the Rope

We'll use another metaphor from Steven Hayes and his colleagues (1999) to examine this type of letting go. Imagine that you're standing near the edge of a wide, bottomless pit. On the opposite side of the pit stands a monster. The monster is made up of all of the thoughts and feelings that you fear and avoid. All of your worries and all of the anxiety associated with them are manifested and concentrated in this looming, dark monster. The monster is holding a long rope that is stretched across the bottomless pit. You are holding onto the other end of the rope. You and the monster are engaged in a bitter tug-of-war. What you are most afraid of is that, if the monster wins, you will be pulled over the edge into the bottomless pit. So you dig in your heels, tighten your grip, and pull with all your might on the rope. This is the struggle with your thoughts and feelings. This is the effort to control your worries and your anxiety. It's exhausting, and the harder you try to win, the stronger the monster seems to become.

Now imagine what would happen if you were to simply let go of the rope. What would it be like if you were able to open your hands and let the rope fall to the ground? The monster would still be there. All of your scary thoughts and feelings would still be there, on the other side of the pit, staring back at you. But your relationship to them would be different. The monster would be there, but your struggling would not. The pit would be there, looming before you, but you would not be at risk of falling into it. You would simply be there, aware of the pit, aware of the monster, and not engaged in a struggle to control or avoid either. This is letting go.

In this metaphor, we have a helpful image of what it means to let go of control. We are not getting rid of painful thoughts or feelings by doing this, but we are changing the nature of our relationship to these thoughts and feelings. "Letting go of the rope" in this way sets the stage for observing and accepting our thoughts and feelings, making room for them in our experience.

Keeping Your Hands Off Anxiety & Worry

Many people associate taking control with the use of their hands. Physically, it is your hands that are most often used to exert control over your environment. In nature, if you were attacked by a predator, you would most likely use your hands to fend it off. On a physical level, therefore, it helps to associate letting go of control with opening your hands. When you imagine yourself letting go of the rope, open your hands. Allowing yourself to be aware of worry and to feel anxiety can further be described as "keeping your hands off" the anxiety or worry. Relaxing your hands and continuing to breathe can be a useful reminder to let go and feel the anxiety, keeping your hands off your feelings and your thoughts.

EXERCISE 5.7:
Hands Off Anxiety and Worry

When you are aware of anxiety and worry:

1. Close your eyes. Focus on your worry thoughts and the feelings that accompany them.

2. Inhale, tightening your fists slightly. Be aware of the tension in your body that signifies your struggle with the anxiety and worry.

3. As you exhale, open your hands slowly, letting go of the struggle with your thoughts and feelings. Think "let go ..."

4. Continue to breathe, observing your worry and anxiety, keeping your hands open and relaxed at your sides, keeping your hands off the anxiety and worry.

5. If you notice yourself tensing up and becoming engaged in struggle or resistance, take another breath, noticing the tension of the struggle or resistance. Then exhale, relaxing your hands more, letting go again. Feel the anxiety that is there, but keep your hands off of it. Observe the thoughts that are there, keeping your hands off of them.

LEANING INTO ANXIETY

Letting go of the effort to control your thoughts and feelings will become easier with practice. While relaxing your muscles and keeping your hands open, it can help to remember to just keep breathing. While interrupting your automatic, instinctual control response is a helpful step toward developing the willingness to feel your feelings and experience your thoughts, it is only the beginning. To move closer to acceptance, it is helpful to actually "lean into" the anxiety that you are feeling.

For anyone who has ever driven on an icy road, the conflict between our instinctual responses and what actually works is familiar. Driving along at a moderate speed, you hit a patch of ice. The car begins to skid to the right. Your instinctual response at this moment might be to slam on the brakes and to turn the steering wheel away from the direction of the skid. This makes sense from a control perspective. You are moving, and you want to stop, so you use the brakes. You are moving too far to the right, so you turn the wheel to the left.

Unfortunately, this response, which would be effective enough on a dry road, does not work so well when driving on ice. What any seasoned Midwestern driver will advise you to do in this situation is to tap the brakes only lightly, and to turn into the skid. This is analogous to letting go of control and leaning into your worry and anxiety. When you feel anxiety increasing, your instincts tell you to step on the brake, to stop the anxiety. As we have discussed, this does not usually work and often leads to even more intense feelings of anxiety. Keeping your hands off anxiety and worry is like keeping your foot off the brake when driving over an icy patch of road. Similarly, the counterintuitive response of leaning into and feeling your feelings of anxiety is much like turning into the skid. It may go against your initial instincts, but unlike pulling away from your feelings or turning away from the skid, it is less likely to result in a spinout.

We can also compare the experience of feeling your feelings to skiing down a hill. One of the challenges for most beginning skiers is the counterintuitive nature of leaning forward when skiing down a steep hill. Our instincts tell us to lean *away* from the downward slope. We want to compensate for the slope of the hill by leaning backwards. This gives us the sense of standing up straight, which we're accustomed to. However, as ski instructors are quick to explain, it is impossible to maintain your balance while moving down the hill unless you are willing to lean forward, leaning *into* the slope of the hill. Similarly, letting go of control and leaning into your feelings of anxiety means being open to feeling whatever you are feeling, even as your instincts tell you to pull away from and to avoid this experience.

LETTING GO & LLAMP

Practicing all of the exercises in this chapter will make it easier for you to let go of the effort to control anxiety and worry when it occurs. Think of these exercises as workouts or training for the actual process of letting go when you are confronted with anxiety and worry. The moment when worry and the feelings that go along with it actually pop up is not the best time to practice any of the letting-go exercises in their entirety. Rather, letting go of control is a more general response that you are developing through the use of the exercises and then applying when worry and anxiety come up.

In the context of the LLAMP approach, you will likely find that specific elements of the exercises are helpful, like relaxing certain muscles, taking a deep abdominal breath, relaxing your hands, or using images of letting go or leaning into anxiety. Remember, the objective is not to become completely relaxed or even to reduce your level of anxiety. Rather, this step is about interrupting the impulse toward control that is part of your automatic response to worry thoughts. This makes room for a new approach to your thoughts and feelings based on acceptance, which we turn to in the next chapter.

CHAPTER SIX

ACCEPT & OBSERVE
WORRY THOUGHTS

At this point, you may be more aware of the different forms that worry takes in your life. By noticing the outcome of your thinking process, you are hopefully able to better distinguish between useful processes like planning or problem solving and nonproductive worry. Recognizing and labeling these thoughts and the feelings and sensations related to them is the first step of the LLAMP approach. Chapter 5 detailed the next step, which is to let go of your initial control response, making room for the steps of acceptance and mindfulness. While these two steps actually happen simultaneously and support one another, we will begin by exploring the concept of acceptance in this chapter and tackle mindfulness in the next.

Acceptance of your worry thoughts and related feelings and sensations involves two parts:

1. Developing a context of willingness for the experience of worry and anxiety by separating your self from your experiences, and

2. Recognizing that your thoughts are not equivalent to the actual things and events that they refer to.

SEPARATING YOUR *SELF* FROM YOUR EXPERIENCE

The story of the man in the gas tank is a reminder of the importance of context for determining our experiences. In chapter 2, we discussed the relationship between worry or anxiety and the desire for control, emphasizing that while control often works well on the outside, when it comes to inside experiences like thoughts and feelings, the more we try to get rid of them, the more likely we are to have them. In chapter 3, the concept of willingness was introduced as an alternative to control, specifically willingness to feel (acceptance) and willingness to act (commitment). You may recall that one way of describing willingness is as a specific context for experiencing your thoughts and feelings. Acceptance is about developing this context of willingness.

Another way to describe willingness is as a new perspective from which to observe your thoughts, feelings, and sensations. Labeling your experience as "worry" and letting go of your impulse toward control sets the stage for this shift, which can also be described as the move from viewing the world *through* your thoughts and feelings to looking *at* your thoughts and feelings. Crucial to making this move is the understanding that you are bigger than your thoughts and feelings.

As mentioned in chapter 4, as a human being, you are thinking all the time. Because of this, it's easy to sometimes have the sense that you *are* your thoughts or feelings. Our language actually reflects and reinforces this perception when we say things like "I *am* frightened" or "I *am* worried." However, the fact is that thoughts and feelings are actually just *part* of your experience at any given time.

For example, right at this moment, in addition to your thoughts and feelings, your experience includes the words on this page, the pages themselves, the binding of the book that you are holding, the room that you're sitting in, the objects that you can observe in your immediate environment, whether your stomach is empty or full, the temperature, and any other people that might be nearby. If you think about it for a moment, you are no more your thoughts and feelings than you are this book or the chair that you're sitting in.

To help with this slightly slippery concept, let's go back to the idea of *context*. One way of understanding the difference between you and your thoughts and feelings is to consider that you as thinker and feeler are the context and that your thoughts, feelings, sensations, this book, your chair, and everything else in your awareness is *content*. The beginning of acceptance of your thoughts and feelings is an awareness of the separate nature of your *self* (context) and your experience (content). This is not only an intellectual or philosophical concept—it is an experience as well. The exercises presented later in this chapter are designed to help you realize the separateness of your self and your experience. In other words, they will help you to shift from operating at the content level of awareness to the context level. Acceptance happens when you are operating at the context level.

The Observer You

"Accept" is an unusual verb. Like all verbs, it is something we do, but unlike active verbs like "run," "sit," "smile," or "touch," "accept" is more passive. In some ways acceptance is more about what we *don't* do (for example, not fighting, or not struggling), but that's not quite it either. As explained above, one part of accepting your experience is an awareness of that experience as separate from your self (experience as content). Perhaps the closest active verb for describing this is "observing." When we are observing something, we are aware of that something as separate from ourselves. The act of observing implies that there is both the *observer* and the *observed*. One way to become aware of yourself as the context for your experience is to observe your experience (as you began to do with the first step of labeling your thoughts, feelings, and sensations) and to identify your self as the observer. We will refer to this as the "Observer You" or "You as Context."

Who is this Observer You? In the most basic sense, it is the you that has been around all of your life, watching and experiencing everything that you have watched and experienced. It is the same you that is reading these words at this moment and processing their meaning. This seems simple enough, but the concept of you can get confusing when we consider how much we change over time and the breadth of our internal and external experiences. Consider what happens when you look at a family photo album filled with pictures of you taken at different ages. Here's a picture of you when you were four-years-old. Here's one taken at age ten. This is you at age fourteen (ouch!). And here you are at twenty. Look at how much you have changed over time: your height, your hair, the way you stand, walk, talk. Even now your body is constantly changing. Not only are you aging, but you gain weight and lose weight, you get sick and then get well again. Yet somehow, through all of these changes, there is some part of you that remains constant. While you may say things like "I feel like a different person," you know that on a literal level, you are the same person now that you were at four or ten. That part of you that was there at age ten, observing and experiencing, is still here now. It is the Observer You. This is the you that transcends not only all of the changes in your body but also the variety of your internal and external experiences. This is you as the context for all of those experiences.

Another way to think of this is to consider the social roles that you fulfill on a daily basis. It starts in the morning while you're driving or riding to work. During this time, you are a commuter. When you get to work, you suddenly become an employee. This is your role until lunchtime, when you grab a bite to eat with a colleague and are a coworker or a friend. After work, you head home where you finish your day by being a parent, a spouse, a child, a roommate, or any combination of these. As you go through your day, moving from one role to another, it's likely that you change in certain ways. Yet, in some essential way, you remain the same. At the end of the day, there is a sense of the continuity of you throughout all of these experiences. This part of you that transcends all of the different roles that you play in your life is the Observer You.

Now consider your thoughts and feelings. Much like changes in the weather, as days and weeks go by, your emotions shift and change. There are moments of happiness, periods of sadness, pangs of guilt, and episodes of anxiety. Similarly, the content of your thoughts is constantly changing. You think about things that need to be done, you think about the relationships in your life, you focus on the task at hand, you ponder what to have for lunch, you remember a favorite song, and you worry. Through all of these changes of thoughts and feelings, your internal experience is constantly changing, yet you, the you that is feeling and thinking all of this, remain the same. The Observer You is the one constant in the equation. Being aware of and identifying with this Observer You provides the perspective on your thoughts and feelings that will make it possible to begin to accept them.

Panning Back: Art vs. Ant

To understand the implications of this shift in perspective, imagine a large abstract painting. The paint has been applied to the canvas very thickly, and when you look at the painting closely, it resembles the mountains and valleys of a topographical map. Now consider the experience of a very tiny ant that is crawling across the painting. From the ant's perspective, this action is like traveling through a strange and treacherous landscape. For the ant, crawling over and through the swirls of paint is like climbing mountains and crossing valleys. If you were the ant, it would be easy to get lost in this strange landscape, and finding your way out of a particular valley or swirling formation would be critical. When you move back from the painting, however, and look at the entire work of art, your experience of these same swirls of paint changes. That particular mountain or valley becomes just one small part of a bigger picture.

You can experience your thoughts and feelings in much the same way. At times, when you are stuck down on the "content" level, you are like the ant. Your thoughts and feelings loom above you like mountains, or you are trapped in them as though they were long, deep valleys. However, if all of these thoughts and feelings are parts of your experience, they are included and contained within a larger context that is you. Therefore, you cannot possibly be the ant. Since you are the context within which all of these thoughts and feelings or swirls of paint are contained, you are more like the art. When you are caught up with the content of your experiences, struggling with worry and anxiety, acceptance involves an awareness that you are the art, not the ant. Shifting from the content or ant perspective to the context or art perspective is a bit like panning back with a movie camera to shift from a close-up to a panoramic perspective. As you begin to observe your thoughts and feelings more objectively, you will develop this ability to "pan back" and gain distance between your self and your experience. This is a crucial part of acceptance.

The Chess Board

Before leaving the distinction between content and context, let's consider one more metaphor from Steven Hayes and his colleagues that illustrates the idea of the Observer You as context for your thoughts and feelings (1999). Imagine a chessboard that extends forever in every direction. On the board, there are white pieces and black pieces. Each of these pieces represents a thought, a feeling, or a sensation. On one side of the board are all of the pieces that we consider "good" and desirable thoughts, feelings, and sensations. On the opposite side are the "bad" pieces. As the game goes on, there is a continuous battle between the good pieces and the bad pieces. Some days it looks like the white pieces are winning. On other days, the black pieces seem to be in the lead. If these pieces are your thoughts, feelings, and sensations, where are *you* in this picture?

Much of the time, you are right down there among the black-and-white pieces. You are invested in the ongoing battle between the good and bad thoughts, feelings, and sensations. When you are operating at this content level, it is crucial that the good pieces win the war. However, this only makes sense if the good pieces are you and the bad pieces are not. However, the bad pieces are content just as much as the good pieces. They are all on the board. So, once again, where is the Observer You in this metaphor? Where is the You as Context? Is it possible that rather than being any of the pieces, and far from being a player who can control any of the pieces, that in fact you are the chessboard itself? Consider for a moment what it would be like if you experienced this game not as a black piece or as a white piece, but as the board that contained all of the pieces all of the time—no matter who was winning. What would it be like to simply be the context for all of these good and bad thoughts, feelings, and sensations, without being so invested in which side happens to be winning at any given moment?

Shifting from the content level (identifying with the good or bad pieces) to the level of You as Context is a move toward acceptance. When you do the exercises presented in this chapter and the next, you will be operating at this context level, as the Observer You.

You Are Bigger Than Your Worries

When you realize that you are not your thoughts, feelings, and sensations (the chess pieces), but in fact you are the context for these (the board), one of the first things you will notice is that you are, in a sense, *bigger* than your internal experiences. You are bigger than your worries. They, in turn, are just one part of your experience rather than all of it. Gaining this perspective is something like what happens when we take a break from watching a movie. Sitting in a darkened theater, when we are focused on the movie, we become engrossed in the story that is unfolding before us. We develop alliances and sympathies with the characters and become emotionally involved in the plot. Suppose, however, that at some point during the movie you were to take a break. Perhaps you decide to go to the lobby for more popcorn. The first thing you do is look away from the screen. You see the people sitting on either side of you. You notice the candy wrappers on the floor and the gum on the back of the seat in front of you. You might look at the walls and ceiling of the theater or notice the slope of the floor. As you walk up the aisle, you see the exit signs over the doors and the glow from the screen reflected on the faces of the audience. Looking over your shoulder once more before you exit, you see the images on the screen and note what is happening in the movie, but you also see the back of everyone's head.

At this point, your relationship to what happens on the screen has changed. You are aware that the characters and events that you were so involved with a moment before are just images projected on a white screen. In a moment, you will be standing in line for popcorn. This shift from being "into" the movie to simply observing the movie as one part of what is going on in the whole theater is similar to the shift from the content level to the context level of your experience. Your worries are much like the images on the screen. By sitting back and observing them as just one part of your experience, your relationship to them changes. Like the person who is only half-watching the movie, it becomes less important what specific images happen to be on the screen at any given time.

This analogy does not imply that your life is not real, only that it is bigger than the specific thoughts, feelings, and sensations that you are aware of at any particular moment. You are not a character in the movie. You are not even the movie. You are the theater. Like any theater, you are capable of featuring all sorts of movies. Recognizing the separation between your self as the theater and your thoughts, feelings, and sensations as the movie will increase your willingness to screen or to accept whatever happens to be playing at any given time.

The Allure of Content

Even when you are able to identify with the Observer You as the context for all of your thoughts, feelings, and sensations, it's easy to get pulled in to the content level, engaging with content in ways that are nonproductive. There are often certain thoughts that we find particularly compelling. Thoughts like "I will always be alone," "I'm unlovable," or "something terrible is going to happen" call out for our attention and involvement. Emotions like anxiety and anger trigger a similar desire for involvement, usually as efforts to control these feelings. On the content level, this involvement can take the form of analytical thinking that leaves us intellectually confused, emotionally depleted, and behaviorally paralyzed.

Engaging with thoughts and feelings in this way can be compared to sorting through scrap metal on a conveyor belt. Imagine that you are standing next to the conveyor belt, and that each piece of sharp, jagged metal is a disturbing worry or an undesirable feeling. Observing it, you may be tempted to reach into the scrap metal as it moves past to try to sort it out or arrange it in a better or safer way. The problem with this level of involvement with the scrap metal is that your bare hands and forearms get scraped and cut. Operating as the Observer You means keeping your hands off of the scrap metal and allowing it to continue on its way unchanged.

ACCEPTANCE EXERCISES I: SEPARATING *SELF* FROM EXPERIENCE

For each of these exercises, it may be easier to make a tape recording of the instructions, and listen to the tape as you do the exercise.

EXERCISE 6.1:
Experiencing the Observer YOU

I. Begin this exercise by closing your eyes. Observe what it is like to close your eyes. Notice that it's just you in there experiencing "eyes closed." You are the observer. You are the context for all that you are aware of. Listen to the sounds that you hear. Notice the physical sensations you are aware of. Observe any thoughts that come to mind. All of this is content. Notice the separate nature of you as context and the sounds, sensations, and thoughts as content.

2. Now open your eyes. Look around at the objects in your immediate environment. As you slowly look at each object, notice the separation between you as the observer and the object that you are observing. Notice that this Observer You is the same you that was just observing all of the components of the experience of eyes closed.

3. Now close your eyes again. Once again observe all that you are aware of with your eyes closed. Notice sounds, notice sensations, notice thoughts. Let yourself be aware that the person observing all of this is the same you that was just observing the objects in your environment when your eyes were open.

4. Open your eyes again. Look around at all of the objects in your immediate environment. Keeping your eyes open, see if you can be aware of both the objects in your environment and the sounds, sensations, and thoughts that you were observing when your eyes were closed. Notice that you are the same you whether your eyes are open or closed. Be aware of yourself as the context for all of your experience: objects, sounds, sensations, and thoughts.

EXERCISE 6.2:
Observing and labeling Content

For this exercise you will need a stack of adhesive sticky notes and a pen.

1. Start by noticing physical sensations in your body. Begin at your feet and slowly work your way up your body.

When you notice a sensation, write a word describing that sensation (tingling, sore, cold, itchy) on a sticky note and stick it to the part of your body where you feel that sensation.

2. Now notice the objects in your environment. Write words that describe some of these objects on sticky notes (lamp, chair, book, plant) and stick the notes on the objects that they describe.

3. Now notice any thoughts that you are aware of. In particular, notice any worries that might be on your mind. Write some of these thoughts on separate sticky notes. Stick the notes up on the walls where you can see them.

4. Look at all of the sticky notes—on your body, on objects in the room, on the walls. Be aware that all of the experiences described on these notes are content. Be aware of the Observer You who created the notes as the context for all of this.

5. Collect all of the notes together, folding them up as small as possible. Put them in your pocket. Notice that you are bigger than all of these elements of your experience. Carry them around in your pocket for the rest of the day.

EXERCISE 6.3:
Observing Worries as Scrap Metal

Close your eyes. Imagine that you are standing next to a conveyor belt. The belt is moving continuously. On the belt are pieces of scrap metal in different shapes and sizes. On each piece of metal is a thought. It may appear as a word or as an image, but each piece of metal carries a thought produced by the thought factory that is your mind. Simply observe each thought as it comes along, notice what it is, then allow it to continue to move slowly past. Then wait for the next thought to come along. Be on the lookout for any worry-related thoughts. In this exercise, you might imagine the scrap metal that holds the worry thoughts as particularly sharp and jagged. This will just help you remember to keep your distance, simply observing the thought and letting it continue on its way. If you notice the impulse to get involved with the scrap metal in any way, to sort it out or to address any of the worries with reassurance, notice that this impulse is itself a thought and let it travel along on the conveyor belt as well.

EXERCISE 6.4: Key Worries

This is an exercise described by Steven Hayes and his colleagues (1999).

1. Make a list of four or five worries that are currently a problem. Write each worry as a thought, trying to capture the worry in a single, short sentence, putting quotes around the statement. Look at your outside/inside monitoring for ideas.

2. Now look at the keys on your key ring. For each of the thoughts on the list, pick one key that you frequently use and assign the thought to that key. Note the key you have assigned to each thought on the list. When you are done, your list will look something like this:

Thought	Key
"What if I get laid off from my job?"	House key
"I wonder if Sue is angry with me."	Car key
"What if this fatigue means I have cancer?"	Key to file cabinet
"Do I look fat in this outfit?"	Storage shed key

3. As you hold up each key, say the thought that goes with that key out loud. Practice this several times until you have memorized which thought goes with which key. As you do this, notice that it is you having each thought. Notice that you can change the sequence of the

thoughts at will by holding different keys. Be aware of the separation that exists between you as the person holding the keys/thoughts and the keys/thoughts themselves.

4. As you go through your day, every time you use one of these keys, allow yourself to think the thought that goes with that key. Notice any feelings that come up when you do this, and allow yourself to feel those feelings. Notice that you are bigger than all of these thoughts and feelings. Think about the fact that you are able to carry these thoughts around with you all day in your pocket or purse.

SEPARATING THOUGHTS FROM THEIR REFERENTS

Remember Irwin and his dangerous thought from chapter 2? Irwin equated the experience of the thought of a head-on collision, something most of us have experienced when driving on a two-lane road, with the experience of an actual head-on collision. This means that he rejected and fought against the thought with the same intensity that he would fight against the threat of an actual collision. This equation of thoughts with the actual things and events the thoughts refer to (their *referents*) is described in ACT terminology as *cognitive fusion*. While most of us know intellectually that thoughts can't harm us, experientially the fusion of thoughts with the reality they are referring to is not uncommon at all. Consider the case of the shark-infested surfer.

The Shark-Infested Surfer

Kelp, a very experienced surfer, spent almost every weekend riding the waves. For years, he had surfed at the same beach. He had always been aware of the fact that he shared the ocean with any number of potentially man-eating sharks; however, this was never cause for alarm. He was not only experienced but also cautious and very safety conscious. Then, in the midst of a summer of exceptionally good surfing, Kelp saw two news reports of shark attacks within the same week. Even though neither of the attacks had occurred anywhere near the section of the coast where he did his surfing, Kelp couldn't help thinking about them as he paddled out into the surf the following Saturday. He noticed that he was much more aware of sounds and movement in the water, and became more tense and wary the farther he got from shore.

Straddling his board and slowly backing into a swell, Kelp felt something brush against his leg. He gasped and almost shouted as he jerked his leg up onto the board, only to find that he had encountered a bit of seaweed. He smiled at his jumpiness but began to think about what it would be like if it were indeed a shark that had scraped past his leg. In spite of himself, he scanned the horizon for any signs of a telltale fin. Of course, this cued the theme music from Jaws in his head. Lying on the board, he could feel his heart beating in his chest. Then, without waiting for a wave, Kelp began to paddle furiously toward the beach. He didn't stop until he had scrambled, dripping and clutching his board, completely out of the water.

Many of us have had an experience similar to Kelp's and would dismiss it as having the jitters or getting freaked out. However, consider the following question. What was it, exactly, that Kelp was so afraid of? Was it being alone in the ocean? Was it the seaweed? If we were to ask Kelp, he might say, "Dude! I was *afraid* of the *sharks!*" The only problem with this answer is that when Kelp was in the water, there were no sharks around. Instead, what was in the water with Kelp, and what he was afraid of and eventually escaped from, was the *thought* of sharks. Kelp's problem is not a fear of sharks. Fear of sharks is not a problem. You are in the water and see a shark, you feel fear, you swim away as fast as possible—no problem. What is a problem, at least for Kelp, is having a fear of the thought of sharks. In order to get back to the surfing that he loves, it isn't necessary for Kelp to overcome his fear of sharks. He only needs to be willing to stay in the water with the thought of sharks. Thankfully, unlike sharks, thoughts have no teeth.

In acceptance and commitment therapy, experientially separating thoughts from the reality that they refer to is called *cognitive defusion*.

It's far easier to accept thoughts when we see them as thoughts. When a thought is particularly alarming, this may be difficult. People who have panic attacks often have the thought "I'm going to die." This sort of thought is part of the panic attack and does not refer to any real threat to the person's life. As a thought, "I'm going to die" is no more dangerous than "I'm going to buy," "I'm going to sigh," or "I'm going to bake a pie." However, on a content level, there is something about "I'm going to die" that makes it harder to regard it as just a thought.

The same is true of thoughts that make judgments about who we are. Defusion can be especially difficult with thoughts like "I'm a loser" or "I'll always be alone." Thoughts like these are like the little man behind the curtain in *The Wizard of Oz*. Dorothy and her friends trembled when they saw what appeared to be a giant head and heard the booming voice saying, "I am Oz, the great and terrible!" What they discovered, however, was that the real wizard was a powerless fraud. Our thoughts can often play a similar trick. They present themselves as real-life threats, saying, "I am dangerous! Fear me!" when, behind the curtain, they are only thoughts.

One thing that can make it easier to see behind the curtain is to change the way we frame these troubling thoughts, making it explicit that they are only thoughts. For example, instead of thinking "I'm going to die," if you were to say to yourself "I'm having the thought that I'm going to die," your experience might be quite different. The same is true for feelings. Instead of "I *am* anxious," try "I am having a feeling of anxiety." Using these distancing phrases can help you to achieve both defusion of the thought from its referent by reminding you that thoughts are only thoughts, and the separation of your self from your experience. When you say to yourself "I am having the thought that I am a loser" or "I am having a feeling of sadness," it is easier to operate at the observer or context level, identifying your thoughts and feelings as thoughts and feelings, or content.

ACCEPTANCE EXERCISES II: COGNITIVE DEFUSION

The remaining exercises in this chapter are designed to help you experience defusion of your thoughts from the reality that they refer to.

EXERCISE 6.5: Playing with your Worries

1. Sit down with pen and paper. Pick one of your worry themes and write it at the top of the page. Allow yourself to worry for several minutes. As you do this, write your thoughts out on the paper. Don't worry about them making sense. When you're done, put all that you have written in quotation marks to remind yourself that these are all just thoughts.

2. Read the thoughts out loud. Start by reading them in your normal voice, then slow your voice down and lower the pitch, like a record playing at the wrong speed. Then speed your voice up, raising the pitch, like a record playing too fast. Listen closely to what this sounds like. Notice what happens to the thoughts as you do this. Does it become more apparent that these are just thoughts?

3. Pick a simple tune, like "Row, Row, Row Your Boat," and sing the thoughts that are on the page. What happens to the thoughts as you do this?

4. Try saying the thoughts as though you were a robot.

5. Say the thoughts in the voice of a cartoon character or with a foreign accent.

6. Standing over the sink, bring a glass of water to your mouth and tilt the glass so that the water covers your lips. Breathing through your nose, say the thoughts into the water, making bubbles as you speak. Listen to the sound of this, and notice what happens to the thoughts.

7. Make a paper airplane or other paper sculpture out of the thought and put it on display.

8. Select another worry theme and repeat the exercise.

EXERCISE 6.6: Rhyming Worries

1. Whenever you notice a worry, try to capture it in a short, single sentence. Say the sentence out loud.

2. Now come up with a completely different, arbitrary worry that rhymes with the original worry thought. For example:

Original Worry	Rhyming Worry
"What if my speech is a failure?"	"What if that peach is a sailor?"
"I might not be able to cope!"	"I might get a mouthful of soap!"
"I probably offended my boss!"	"I think I upended the sauce!"
"What if the airplane crashes?"	"What is this pain in my lashes?"

3. Try replacing the original worry with the rhyming worry thought. Try to think it with the same sense of urgency or alarm that you gave to the original worry.

4. Notice that the original worry and the rhyming worry are both thoughts, and that as such, the original worry poses no more of a threat than the rhyming worry.

EXERCISE 6.7: Let's Put on a Show!

This exercise is especially helpful for defusing "What if ..." worries and worries about social situations.

1. When you have identified a "What if ..." worry, allow yourself to consider what might happen if the event you

are worried about actually came to pass. Let yourself imagine the worst-case scenario played out to the bitter end.

2. Gather a variety of small, everyday objects together (for example, a spoon, a pencil, a lightbulb, a tennis ball, etc.)

3. Assign each object a role in the worst-case scenario that you have just imagined, and put on a play!

4. Act out the scenario from start to finish, using the objects to play the parts of everyone involved. For example, if you are worried that your boss was offended by a comment you made earlier today and that he might fire you because of it, you might choose a coaster to be you and the TV remote to play the role of your boss. Act out the scene where you make the comment, making the coaster "talk" to the TV remote. Then skip ahead to the next scene, where the TV remote fires the coaster, etc.

5. Notice what happens to your worries as you act them out. Try repeating the same scene but with all of the parts being played by pieces of fruit or by past presidents as depicted on coins and bills.

Defusion of Evaluations and Judgments

A related type of fusion that we all experience is the fusion of our evaluations and judgments with the people, things, and events that we apply them to. The ability to evaluate and judge people, things, and experiences is unique to human beings, and like many other things unique to our species, it's related to our ability to use language. As a language machine, your mind produces evaluations and judgments and then attaches these to people, objects, or experiences in the real world. You may then proceed as though these judgments were actually part of the object, person, or experience that your mind attached them to. Defusion helps you to recognize the difference between those qualities that exist in objects, people, or experiences and the judgments that actually reside within you.

For example, is there really any such thing as an "ugly" sofa? The sofa might have certain attributes that belong to it. For example, the fabric might be printed with large gold flowers. It might have thick, green fringe. It might be lumpy and have large knobby wooden legs with brass studs on them. The ugly part of the sofa, however, lies in the eye of the observer. In a certain living room in a certain part of the country at a certain time in the 1970s, this same piece of furniture might be a beautiful sofa. The same is true of judgments you make about yourself, others, or experiences.

It is perfectly normal for our minds to produce judgments and evaluations. This is what the mind does. This only becomes problematic when we then react to these judgments and evaluations as though they are real, unchangeable aspects of the world (as opposed to verbal labels that we have applied to the world). When these labels are negative, we can then begin to feel oppressed by these negative "attributes" of people, things, and events that are not really attributes but instead are judgments that reside within us.

Judgments and evaluations are most oppressive when we apply them to ourselves. For example, when you consider all of the worrying that you do and the avoidance that accompanies it, you likely have certain judgments that you attach to yourself. You might think something like "I'm pathetic." When you look at this label more closely, it begins to look almost arbitrary. When you say "I'm pathetic," what does this really mean? Could you prove it to be true? Consider these other statements. Are they true or false as applied to you? Could you prove them to be true or false?

"I'm tall."

"I'm short."

"I have brown hair."

"I speak softly."

"I often procrastinate."

"I often feel anxious."

Now consider the statement "I'm pathetic." Do you know this to be true or false in the same way that you know these other statements to be true or false? Could you prove it with the same certainty? All of the statements listed above are descriptions. They are qualities that are inherent in you or your behavior. "Pathetic," on the other hand, is simply a word that expresses judgment. It doesn't actually *describe* anything real.

EXERCISE 6.8: Evaluate the Room

This exercise is designed to help you to identify judgments and evaluations and to defuse them from the things they refer to. You will need a stack of adhesive sticky notes.

1. Consider several objects in the room one at a time. Come up with a judgment or evaluation of each object and write it on a sticky note. Attach the judgment to the object. For example, you might attach the judgment "harsh" to the lamp, "pretty" to a picture on the wall, or "unsettling" to a newspaper. (Note that this is different from what you did in exercise 6.2. In that exercise you were writing descriptions on the sticky notes. While descriptions are attributes that are part of the object, judgments are created and assigned exclusively by you.)

2. Come up with a judgment about yourself as well. Apply a sticky note with that judgment to your clothing.

3. Look at all of the judgments. Allow yourself to recognize that these are thoughts produced by your mind.

4. Collect all of the notes together and mix them up. Arbitrarily reassign the judgments, sticking the notes on all of the same objects in the room, including yourself, but in a random order.

5. Look at each object, and try to apply the newly assigned judgment to that object. See if it's possible to actually regard each object in the light of your new judgment. For example, is it possible to see the newspaper as "pretty" in some way or yourself as "harsh"?

6. Notice that judgments are somewhat arbitrary, and that they are not permanently attached to what is being judged.

7. Remove the notes and again randomly assign them, this time to objects that have not been judged before or to objects in another room. See if it is possible to actually judge each object according to the judgment you have attached to it. Notice that even judgments that are arbitrarily assigned can be powerful in shaping our experience.

ACCEPTANCE & MINDFULNESS

The acceptance step of the LLAMP approach (separating your self from your thoughts and your thoughts from their referents) works together with the next step, mindfulness. While they are presented here as separate steps, they are in some ways two sides of a single coin. As you have been doing the exercises in this chapter, you have been practicing mindfulness of your thoughts by observing and experiencing them in a defused way. The next chapter looks at mindfulness more closely and how it can help to connect us to the present moment.

CHAPTER SEVEN

MINDFULNESS OF THE PRESENT MOMENT

Acceptance involves mindfulness, and mindfulness involves acceptance. Separating your self from your experience and recognizing thoughts as separate from the things and events they refer to both involve the mindful observation of your experience. Mindfulness means not only observing but being open to everything that you are experiencing in the present moment (thoughts, feelings, sensory experiences) in a defused, nonjudgmental, and compassionate way. This means seeing thoughts as thoughts without getting carried away by or pulled into them on the content level.

You actually began practicing mindfulness with the first LLAMP step of labeling your thoughts. Labeling thoughts requires an awareness of what you are thinking. Accepting our thoughts and feelings requires that we be aware of them as separate from our selves and as separate from their referents. Mindfulness and the previous LLAMP step, acceptance, both involve defusion. To this extent, the two concepts overlap and complement one another. Being mindful of the present moment is one step in the LLAMP approach to worry, but it is also a skill that can enhance many areas of your life. Like any other skill, your ability to be mindful will improve with practice.

THE PRESENT MOMENT

If you consider the things that you are most often upset about, you will likely find that the majority of those things either occurred in the past or are waiting to possibly occur in the future. When you are depressed or distracted by ruminations, your thoughts are usually focused on events that occurred in the past. At the moment that you're thinking about them, these events are only memories. The largest part of your anxiety and worry is most likely focused on events that may or may not occur in the future. At the moment you are imagining these events, they are merely imagined images of possibilities. While our awareness of the twin illusions of past and future are often characterized by pain and anxiety, the present moment is available to us in a different way. When we are able to exist more fully in the present moment, we often find less cause for concern.

Take this moment for example. You are reading this book. Where are you right now? Are you terribly uncomfortable physically? Are you extremely warm or extremely cold? Are you in physical pain? Are you experiencing extreme hunger or thirst? If the answer to these questions is no, then the present moment is probably an acceptable place to be. Mindfulness means being willing to exist more fully in the present moment. When we do this, we often find that the present moment holds more peace and contentment than either the past or the future. Many people experience this grounding in the present moment when they engage in certain activities. For example, certain sports that require focus and full involvement of the body's senses are one way of becoming more mindful of the present moment. Other examples would be playing a musical instrument, cooking a gourmet meal, or grooming a beloved pet.

This focus on the present moment does not mean that we can't have thoughts about the past or future when we are practicing mindfulness. Our present moment awareness will often include thoughts about the past or future. When we observe these thoughts mindfully, however, it is with the recognition that they are only thoughts, and that the past and future that they refer to are not real *right now*. This involves cognitive defusion (seeing thoughts as thoughts), but it also requires awareness of where we are and what is going on now. The exercises in this chapter will not only help you to develop more awareness of your thoughts and feelings but will also help you to be aware of the sounds you hear, the things you see, and the flavors, scents, and other sensations that make up your complete experience of the present moment. When you're practicing mindfulness, you will still have thoughts that can be labeled as "worry," but you are less likely to be carried away by these thoughts into the past or future. When worries do carry you away from the present, mindfulness can bring you back.

MINDFULNESS & THE SENSES

One way to connect with the present moment is through our senses. Immediate experiences like sounds, sights, smells, tastes, and bodily sensations exist only in the present. Focusing on them can bring us into contact with the current moment and help to keep us there. Usually as we go about our daily lives, we are not consciously aware of much that we see, hear, smell, taste, or touch. When we are practicing mindfulness, we pay more attention to our experience of the world as we contact it through our senses. Often, the only time we bring this kind of focus to sensory experiences is when we are describing, judging, or evaluating those experiences.

When we look at an article of clothing that we are thinking about buying, for example, we may be more aware of the colors and patterns that we are seeing, or the feel of the fabric, as we attach judgments to these elements like "attractive," "gaudy," or "comfortable." When we taste something new, we are more attentive to the sense of taste than when we eat foods that we are familiar with, but we are also evaluating the taste and deciding whether or not we like what we are tasting. Mindfulness is about approaching these sensory experiences with the goal of simply experiencing them, without an investment in judging or evaluating them. When we practice mindfulness, these judgments still come up, but they are regarded in a defused manner, simply as thoughts that our mind has produced. We can experience the judgment as just another part of our experience, having the thoughts without buying them.

Sounds

Listening to the sounds that we hear can be a powerful way to access the present moment. Sitting in a room with your eyes closed, you can hear distant sounds from other rooms or out of doors. You can hear the sounds that are in the room with you: the ticking of a clock or the hum of a ventilation system. When things are very quiet, you can even hear the rustling, gurgling, and pounding sounds of your own body, along with occasional buzzing and ringing within your ears, sounds that have no outside origin. All of these sounds, as you are hearing them, exist only in the present moment.

EXERCISE 7.1: Listening

Close your eyes. For several minutes, listen closely to everything that you hear. Notice all of the sounds that you hear outside of the room, in the room, and in your body. When you hear a sound and notice yourself thinking about what made the sound, notice that thought, and bring your attention back to the sound. Try to stay with the sounds themselves without being carried away to their origins. If there is a continuous sound, listen for changes in the sound. Notice that as you are listening, you are focused on what you're experiencing *right now*. If you have any judgments about the sounds you hear, notice these and bring your focus back to the sounds themselves.

Sights

Vision is a powerful way of accessing the world around us. Yet, though we have our eyes open most of the day, there is a great deal that we don't see. Most of the time, we use vision in a very utilitarian manner. We use visual information to navigate from place to place, to coordinate physical and mechanical operations on our environment, and to access information in the form of symbols. We see, but our focus is on the meaning of what we see. We are looking, but we are concerned with *why* we are looking, where we are going, or what we are doing besides looking. Mindful seeing is seeing for seeing's sake. When we see mindfully, we are not invested in judgments like "beautiful" or "ugly," though these thoughts may be present. We are experiencing color and shape as experience, not as a means to some other end.

EXERCISE 7.2: Looking

Close your eyes for a few moments, allowing yourself to relax. When you open your eyes take a good look at the room that you're sitting in. Look at the walls, the windows, the doors. Look at the rugs or carpet; look at the furniture. Look at all of the objects in the room. Notice the many colors that you see. Notice the shapes of the objects. See how the different surfaces reflect the light. Notice the shadows of objects. See how many details you can see that you have never noticed before. If you are aware of judgments or other thoughts about what you see, notice this, and bring your focus back to your immediate experience of colors and shapes in the present moment.

Scents

As human beings, perhaps the sense that is most taken for granted is the sense of smell. Other mammals get the vast majority of their information about the world through scents. Human beings also get a great deal of information from scents, even though much of it is ignored. In the absence of visual cues, scents as much as sound can help us to know where we are. We are often alerted to changes in our immediate environment by smells before these changes are registered by any of our other senses. We know that something is burning before we see the smoke or flames, we discern that the person sitting next to us on the bus is a smoker, and we know what's for dinner, all by using our sense of smell. Yet, unless the stimulus is exceptionally powerful, we often ignore what we are smelling.

Perhaps since we make such limited use of scents for functional purposes, we may approach them with more mindfulness than we bring to other sensory experiences. When we smell a flower, or scented candles, fresh sheets, or the skin of a loved one, we usually do so for the pure experience of the fragrance, not to accomplish something else. These are experiences that bring us fully into the present moment.

EXERCISE 7.3: Smelling

1. Start with the medicine cabinet in your bathroom. With your eyes closed, smell each grooming product that you find there, one item at a time: toothpaste, mouthwash, deodorant, hair gel, lotions, creams, etc. Allow yourself to focus only on what you are smelling right now. If you find yourself judging the scent as "good" or "bad," simply observe that judgment without buying it, and refocus on the actual experience of smelling.

2. Now move on to the kitchen. Take out several spices, fresh fruits or vegetables, sauces, or preserves. With your eyes closed, smell each in turn. Allow yourself to be fully present to each fragrance as you are smelling it.

3. Try more subtle scents now. Smell the palm of your hand. Smell the back of your hand. Smell your shoulder. Smell the pages of this book. Smell the throw pillows on the sofa, the sheets on the bed, and the clothes in your closet. Go outside and smell a leaf, a flower, the earth. Let yourself experience these odors without investment in judgments or analysis. Simply experience the sensations offered, allowing yourself to participate more fully in the present moment.

Touch

Another sense that commonly goes unappreciated is the sense of touch. You are probably led by your sense of touch in selecting experiences that you might not readily identify as touch related. For example, the choice to wear your oldest, most broken-in pair of blue jeans or to designate a particular chair as your favorite is guided primarily by your sense of touch. When you enjoy experiences like a warm bath, a hug, or walking barefoot through the grass, you are reveling in the sensations of touch. These sensations can help you to make contact with the present when you hold them in the center of your awareness. Your skin, in addition to separating your inside from the outside, is covered with touch receptors. An unexpected touch from the outside can set off alarms inside your body. New and novel touch gets the most attention, while touch that is constant and enduring, like the weight of your clothing, becomes background. Your fingertips are the most sensitive centers of touch. With them you tentatively explore your most immediate environs to determine what is hot or cold, wet or dry, rough or smooth, hard or soft, sticky or not sticky. While you can be mindful of touch all over your body, it is easiest to be mindful of what you feel with your fingertips. Since your touch sensors quickly habituate to constant pressure, you can be most mindful of touch when you keep your fingertips slowly moving, feeling the changing sensations that mark each moment of awareness.

EXERCISE 7.4: Touching

1. Start with this book. Close your eyes and allow your fingers to explore the book. Feel the pages. Notice the different sensations of moving your finger across a single page and moving your finger over the edges of several pages. Feel the spine and the cover. Notice the difference between the texture of the pages inside the book and the cover on the outside. Hold the book in your palm and feel its weight on your hand. Flip through the pages with one hand, and feel the slight breeze produced with the fingers of the other hand.

2. Find a comfortable place to sit or lie down. Close your eyes and feel the texture of the furniture or the floor that is supporting you. Move your fingertips very slowly, noticing any changes in the materials that you are feeling. If you are touching fabric, notice whether your fingers glide over it smoothly or if the ridges of your fingertips catch on the weave. If you are touching wood or plastic, notice the temperature of this surface and any irregularities or distinguishing features.

3. Hold an ice cube in your fist as you stand over the sink. Close your eyes and focus on the sensation of the ice in

your hand. Continue to hold the ice cube as you feel it begin to melt. Feel the drops of cold water dripping from between your fingers and running down your hand. Drop the ice cube into the sink, and notice how the sensation of cold lingers in the skin of your hand.

Taste

As something that we have done every day of our lives, eating, like breathing, can be exceedingly ordinary and mindless. At other times, however, the sense of taste can bring great joy. The sensations associated with eating actually include a combination of touch and smell as well as taste. Our experience of food is determined as much by its texture, consistency, and odor as by its taste. After the fingertips, our tongue is our most sensitive organ of touch. The practice of mindful eating, described below, emphasizes all elements of the eating experience. To be mindful of taste specifically, it helps to slow or stop the act of chewing. The taste buds are more specialized than touch sensors. They are more or less responsive to specific tastes like sweet, sour, bitter, or salty depending on where they are located on the tongue. Tasting mindfully, we allow food to sit on our tongue, to melt in our mouths, simply observing the changes in flavor and intensity. Swallowing, we are mindful of aftertastes.

EXERCISE 7.5: Tasting

I. Put a small piece of chocolate in your mouth. Hold it on your tongue without chewing it. With your mouth closed, allow the chocolate to slowly melt. Notice the changes in taste as it does so. Spread the melted chocolate over the surface of your tongue, observing the changing intensity of the taste sensations. When the chocolate is completely melted, allow yourself to swallow. Notice the flavors that linger in your mouth after swallowing. Where in your mouth are you most aware of the lingering taste of chocolate?

2. Take a small sip of juice or any flavored beverage, and hold it in your mouth. Starting at the tip of your tongue, slowly move the beverage toward the back of your tongue, holding it for a moment on the tip, then center, then at the back. Notice the changes in taste as the beverage moves from the tip to the back of your tongue.

3. Put a drop of lemon juice on the tip of your finger and touch it to the tip of your tongue. Now put a drop of lemon juice on the very back of your tongue. Then try the same thing on each side of your tongue. Notice the different flavors that you experience on each part of your tongue.

MINDFULNESS OF COMPLEX EXPERIENCES

The preceding exercises emphasize mindfulness of specific, individual experiences. More often, however, our moments are characterized by layers of experience. We are all capable of being aware of more than one thing at a time. For example, as you are reading this, it is possible for you to be aware of the roof of your mouth. You may not have been aware of the roof of your mouth all day, but with a little effort, it's possible to be acutely aware of the roof of your mouth even as you read the rest of this sentence. When we practice mindfulness, it is common for our awareness to flow from one aspect of experience to another, but it is also possible to be simultaneously aware of different aspects or layers of experience.

EXERCISE 7.6: Taste plus Touch

1. Put a pinch of granulated sugar in your mouth. Hold it on your tongue with your mouth closed. Focus on your taste experience as the sugar dissolves. Observe how the taste changes. Try to notice when the taste becomes most intense and the moment when the intensity begins to decline. Observe the sweetness as it fades away.

2. Taking another pinch, hold the sugar between the tip of your tongue and the roof of your mouth. Feel the grittiness of the sugar as it presses against the roof of your mouth. Feel the grains pressing on your tongue. This time, see if you can observe both the sweet taste and the gritty feeling of the sugar. Can you notice the taste and the texture of the sugar at the same time? Watch for the exact moment when the sugar grains dissolve. Can you observe the sweetness as it intensifies and fades away at the same time you are observing the grittiness as it changes?

EXERCISE 7.7: Listening Plus Looking

You can do this exercise either outdoors or indoors. An ideal outdoor setting would be a garden or park that has elements of nature to look at. In this setting, you will need a Walkman or an MP3 player with headphones. Indoors, select a painting (abstracts work well) or several objects that you enjoy looking at, and get comfortable near your stereo.

1. Select a long piece of music or several pieces without words. Sit comfortably in view of flowers and plants if you are outdoors, or the selected painting or objects if you are indoors.

2. Close your eyes. Begin by listening to the music. Focus on the different sounds that you hear that combine to make the experience of music. See if you can pick out individual instruments. Try not to get "carried away" by the music, staying with what you are hearing in each moment. If you notice associations or thoughts triggered by the music or judgments about the music, acknowledge these and then bring your attention back to the sounds that you're hearing right now.

3. When you are able to maintain a focus on the music, open your eyes. Continuing to stay with the music you are hearing in a mindful way, focus on what you see in front of you. Allow yourself to be fully mindful of both

the sights that you're seeing and the sounds you're hearing. Observe any interaction between your experience of the sounds and your experience of the sights. Do these elements of your experience begin to merge or combine in any way?

EXERCISE 7.8: A Warm Bath

There are countless elements of sensation that make up the experience of taking a warm bath. From the moment we turn on the tap, the room fills with sounds, scents, and changes in temperature and humidity.

1. Sit comfortably beside the tub. As the bath water is running, slowly add a little bath oil or bubble bath. Notice any changes in the color of the water. Watch the movement of the water as it fills the tub.

2. Closing your eyes, listen to the sound of the tap running. Allow your awareness to stay with the white noise of the splashing water.

3. Notice the fragrances that are present. The scent of the bath, the scent of nearby soap, the plastic scent of the shower curtain, the scent of steam in the air.

4. When the bath is ready, turn off the water and listen to the quiet that follows the sound of splashing.

5. Step into the bath very, very slowly. As you lower first one foot and then the other into the tub, focus on the sensations of the warm water. Feel the hard surface of the tub underfoot. Stand for a moment with your eyes closed, and see if you can sense the line of the water around your ankles. Notice the difference between the part of your foot that is beneath the water and the part above the water, and observe the line where water and air meet on your skin.

6. Slowly lower yourself into the water, observing the changing sensations all over your body. Pause at

comfortable intervals, noticing which parts of your body are wet and which parts are dry.

7. Settle fully into the water and close your eyes. See if you can be mindful of the water and air touching your skin while also being aware of the sounds in the room. Listen to the drips and gentle splashes as you move about. Also, notice the fragrances again. Allow yourself to be aware of the touch of the water, the sounds, and the smells all at once. Notice how these sensations combine and overlap to form a whole experience of bathing.

8. Gently splash water on your arms and over your chest and face, focusing on the sensations, the temperature, the feeling of water running and dripping across your skin. Try to feel these things while staying present to the scents and sounds that accompany the movement of the water.

9. With a washcloth or sponge, drip water over your head, your chest, your arms.

10. Keeping your eyes open, slide down so that your ears are submerged. Notice the changes in sounds as your ears move from being above to being below the water. Notice any interaction between this change in hearing and your experience of seeing and looking.

11. After soaking for a while, slowly get out of the tub. Notice the change in the temperature of your skin as you leave the tub. Again sitting comfortably beside the tub, towel off slowly and mindfully as the water drains away. Feel the warmth and softness of the towel against your skin, noticing that the experience continues. Listen to the different sounds the water makes as it leaves the tub. When the last of the water has emptied down the drain, notice the quiet that follows. Notice how your body feels, allowing yourself to rest in the present moment.

MINDFULNESS OF YOUR BODY

Being aware of your body can give you a sense of being more fully present in the here and now. No matter where you go in life, your body travels with you. By focusing on your body as a physical fact, something that has mass and weight and currently exists in a specific place, it's possible to become more grounded in your awareness of the present moment. One way to do this is by scanning your body from your feet all the way up to the top of your head, as in the following exercise. This is a different exercise from the tensing and relaxing exercise in chapter 5. In that exercise, the goal was to change your body from a state of tension to a state of relaxation. In this exercise, the objective is simply to observe the body, not to change it. If you observe tension as you do the body scan, simply notice the tension and move on. As a mindfulness exercise, the body scan is about observing and accepting your experience of your body, without making any efforts to alter it.

EXERCISE 7.9: Body Scan

Begin by doing this exercise very slowly. Initially, the entire exercise should take from fifteen to twenty minutes. Eventually, you can do the exercise more quickly as preparation for the exercises that follow.

1. Sit comfortably with your eyes closed, and allow yourself to breathe slowly and deeply for several minutes.

2. Bring your attention to your toes. Notice all of the toes on your left foot—the big toe, the little toe, and all of the toes in between. Notice the toes on your right foot— big, little, and all of the toes in between.

3. Now bring your attention to your feet. Notice your left foot, then your right. Now notice both feet at the same time. Be aware of the bottoms of your feet, the ball, the arch, the heel. Notice the sides and tops of your feet. See if you can feel the pressure of your socks or shoes where they make contact with your feet.

4.   Notice your ankles, the inside of your ankles, and the outside.

5.   Notice your lower legs. Be aware of any tension in your lower legs. Simply note this and move on.

6.   Be aware of your knees, the tops of your knees, and the area behind your knees.

7.   Notice your upper legs. Be aware of any tension in your upper legs and notice where they make contact with the surface you're sitting on.

8.   Be aware of your buttocks and your lower back. Notice any strain or tension in this area. Be aware of where your buttocks and lower back are supported by the chair or the floor.

9.   Notice your middle and upper back. Simply acknowledge any tension you might feel in this area, observing and accepting these feelings.

10.   Now bring your attention to your upper arms, left and right, noticing where they rest beside your body.

11.   Notice your lower arms, your wrists, and your hands. Notice what your hands are touching and what you are able to feel with them.

12.   Now bring your attention to your neck. See if you can feel the muscles on either side of your neck, your throat, and the back of your neck.

13.   Be aware of your face. Notice the muscles around your mouth and your jaw muscles. Notice the area around your eyes, and notice your forehead. Note any tension you might feel in your face, simply observing it and moving on.

14.   Notice your scalp. Notice the muscles that cover your scalp and any sensations that you might feel on the back of your scalp and at the very top of your scalp.

15.   Now allow your awareness to expand to encompass your head, your torso, and your legs and feet. Be aware of

your entire body as a unified whole. Continue to breathe, slowly and deeply. Simply observe your body as a solid object supported by the chair or the floor, being aware that you are right here, right now.

Mindfulness & Breathing

One aspect of your immediate experience that is always readily available to you is the experience of your own breathing. You have been breathing all of your life. Since it occurs inside your body, breathing is a very personal experience. It's an experience that you have access to even with your eyes closed, in a dark room, with no sounds, no scents, no tastes. All breaths, with the exception of our first one and last one, come in pairs. We breathe in and then we breathe out. Since we do it all day long, we are usually not aware of our breathing. Since it is occurring right *now*, your breath is an ideal focal point when you want to be mindful of the present moment.

EXERCISE 7.10: Following Your Breath

1. Sit in a comfortable position and close your eyes. Allow yourself to breathe slowly and deeply through your nose.

2. As you inhale, see if you can feel the movement of air as it flows past your nostrils. Focus on the area around your nostrils for several breaths until you are able to feel the movement of air there as it enters and leaves your body.

3. Now notice the flow of air as it moves higher into your nasal cavity, past the area behind your eyes. You might notice a sensation of coolness behind your eyes as you breathe in.

4. Now see if you can feel the air as it moves into your windpipe, at the back of your throat. You might experience your breath here as a faint tickling at the very back of your tongue.

5. On the next inhale, notice your breath as it moves into your chest. You may feel a slight pressure in the center of your chest as your lungs expand.

6. Finally, see if you can feel your breath all the way down in your belly. See if you can feel your belly expanding as you inhale and relaxing as you exhale.

7. Continue to breathe slowly and deeply. At what point in your body are you most aware of the air as it enters and leaves your body? Let your attention focus on this point, observing your breath for several minutes.

EXERCISE 7.11: Watching Your Breath

Start by spending ten minutes on this exercise. If you're worried about losing track of the time, set a timer.

1. Sitting in a comfortable position, close your eyes and allow yourself to breathe slowly and deeply.

2. Find the one spot that you identified in exercise 7.10 where you are most aware of your breath as it enters and leaves your body.

3. Focusing on this one spot, observe each breath as it enters and leaves your body. Stay focused only on this breath and this moment.

4. If you notice that your mind is wandering, gently bring the focus back to the current breath. Simply observe this breath, this moment.

5. Be aware of any thoughts or judgments you may have, especially about your performance. If you notice the thought "I'm not doing this right" or "this is difficult," simply observe the thought, then bring your focus back to your breath.

Mindfulness & Your Beating Heart

An even more personal experience of the present moment is the sensation of your own heart beating. We are most aware of our heartbeat when it is faster and harder than usual. With practice, however, it is possible to feel your resting heartbeat by sitting quietly and observing. Most people experience this as a slow, rhythmic pulsing in the chest, but you may also feel your heartbeat as a pulse in other parts of your body.

EXERCISE 7.12:
Feeling Your Heart Beating

Start by spending ten minutes on this exercise. If you're worried about losing track of the time, set a timer.

1. Sitting in a comfortable position, close your eyes and allow yourself to breathe slowly and deeply.

2. Start by focusing on your breathing as you did in the last exercise. After several breaths, sit very quietly and notice the center of your body.

3. After a while, you may be able to feel a faint, rhythmic pulsing from within your body. Most people feel this most strongly in the center of the chest or just above the diaphragm. Other people feel this pulsing more easily in their neck or in their lower arms. Some people are able to hear the beating of their heart, but many experience it as a silent pulsing motion inside the body.

4. Simply observe your heart beating. As you do so, if you notice thoughts, feelings, or other sensations, acknowledge these and gently bring your focus back to the beating of your heart.

MINDFULNESS OF THOUGHTS & FEELINGS

Our senses help us to connect to the present moment because the sensory information that is available to us exists only in the here and now. Being mindful of thoughts and feelings in the present moment can be more challenging. When we experience thoughts about the past or the future in a fused way, we are drawn away from the present moment. Mindfulness of sensory experiences or of our breathing or heartbeat can bring us back to the present moment. This practice allows us to observe our thoughts and feelings in a defused way, as another aspect of our experience in the present moment, like our breathing or our heartbeat. The defusion exercises in the previous chapter were also exercises in mindfulness. When we are mindful of our thoughts, we observe and experience them as thoughts. All of the exercises in the previous chapter—designed to facilitate awareness by helping you to experience thoughts and feelings on a context level, where you are the context, and the thoughts and feelings are content—are particularly relevant when it comes to being mindful of your thoughts and feelings.

EXERCISE 7.13: Watching Your Thoughts as a Slide Show

Begin with exercise 7.11, sitting quietly, and focusing on your breathing. Watch your breathing for several minutes. When you are aware of yourself as an observer, watching your breathing, allow yourself to notice that you are having thoughts. Imagine your thoughts projected on a large screen, like a slide show in a darkened room. As you observe the screen, you will notice that thoughts come and go. You might observe your thoughts as images, memories, or words on the screen. When you are aware of a thought, let it go and wait for the next thought to appear on the screen. After a while, you may find the thoughts coming and going in a rhythmic way, just as the images change automatically in a slide show.

Mindfulness & Judgments

Observing your thoughts in the present moment, you are likely to notice that a number of those thoughts are judgments or evaluations. For example, if you are looking at a tree, you might have the thought that it is a "beautiful" tree or a "strong" tree. It's very common to experience judgments about ourselves when we are mindful, particularly about how well we are doing in our efforts to practice mindfulness. These thoughts can be especially difficult to experience in a defused way, and it is often very tempting to get more involved with them.

Mindfulness does not mean an end to judgments—it simply means recognizing and labeling them as judgments and experiencing them in a defused way. When we are mindful of our thoughts, we will notice that we have judgments, but when we are mindful and accepting, we are less likely to buy those judgments.

EXERCISE 7.14:
Eating Food You Don't Like

Pick a specific food that you generally avoid eating because you do not like its taste or texture. Slowly and mindfully take a bite of the food. Simply observe the taste, the texture, and the scent, being mindful of the whole experience of eating this food. Notice also any judgments or evaluations that come to mind as you slowly chew the food. If you notice negative thoughts like "this is disgusting" or "I hate the taste of this," simply notice these evaluative thoughts, labeling them as judgments, and be aware of them as just another part of your experience. See if it is possible to experience the judgmental thoughts without buying them.

EXERCISE 7.15: A Cold Shower

While taking a shower, slowly turn off the hot water. Notice how the water feels on your skin as it slowly becomes colder and colder. Notice any judgments or reactions you have to the change in temperature. If you notice yourself pulling back or otherwise avoiding the cold water, notice this, and then move into the stream of cold water, observing the resistance and any evaluative thoughts you have about the shower, or about yourself. Practice being willing to experience these thoughts along with the sensation of coldness while also being willing to remain standing in the cold water.

Compassion

The mindful stance of being nonjudgmental can also be described as having compassion. Whether we are talking about judging our experience, judging others, or judging ourselves, when we approach something or someone with compassion, we suspend that judgment. Most of us find it easy to feel compassion for small children. When we see a child who is frightened or angry, we are often more likely to respond with empathy and understanding than with criticism. When we see a child who has trouble doing something in spite of a concerted effort, most of us respond with compassion and patience rather than with scoffing or scolding. One goal of mindfulness is to approach ourselves and our experiences with this same sense of compassion. This is especially true when it comes to your judgments about how "well" you are doing when it comes to practicing mindfulness. When you first begin to sit and observe your breathing or your heartbeat, you will likely find that your mind wanders. This is what the mind does. Responding to this with compassion is a crucial aspect of mindfulness.

Shopping with Lucinda

Imagine that you are in a shopping mall with your niece Lucinda, who is three years old. As you walk through the mall, you have the specific goal of getting to the parking lot, finding your car, and going home. Lucinda, however, does not share your single-mindedness. Lucinda is in an energetic mood and is by nature very curious. As the two of you walk through the mall, she strays into almost every store that you pass. Taking you by the hand, she says "Look at this!" and "Oh, what is that thing?" How would you want to respond to Lucinda?

One response would be to completely indulge her every whim, spending as much time in each store as she wishes. In this case, you may never get to the parking lot. Another response would be to take her firmly by the hand and drag her purposefully along, giving her little arm a firm jerk whenever she makes a move toward one of the stores. A compassionate response, however, would be to give Lucinda your attention, acknowledging the things she points out to you and briefly responding to her simple questions, all the while carefully steering her out of each store and toward the parking lot.

When practicing mindfulness of your thoughts, it helps to take a similar approach. As you notice your mind wandering off in the direction of a particular thought, acknowledge the thought ("Yes, Lucinda. I see that"), and then gently bring yourself back to the present moment.

Just as you would want to be compassionate with Lucinda, it is important that you not respond to your mind's wandering in a punishing way. This compassion is part of acceptance. Accepting your thoughts and feelings also means accepting yourself. Becoming critical and judgmental when you notice your mind wandering is like jerking little Lucinda's arm and shouting at her: "Stop that! Can't you see we're trying to get to the parking lot? What's wrong with you?" This type of judgment tends to shut down and derail our efforts at mindfulness.

PRACTICING MINDFULNESS

While the exercises presented so far are a good introduction to mindfulness, to become more in touch with your experience from moment to moment and to experience your thoughts and feelings in a more defused and accepting way takes time and practice. You can use any of the exercises presented so far as often as you like to work on developing mindfulness in the context of specific experiences like taking a bath or listening to music. Perhaps the best way to approach mindfulness, however, is to set aside specific times to practice mindfulness every day. One way to do this is through the regular practice of meditation. You can also incorporate mindfulness into the basic activities that you engage in on a daily basis, like walking or eating.

Mindful Sitting

Most spiritual and philosophical traditions encourage quiet time for mindful observation or meditation. Some people refer to this observation of your own experience in the present moment as "mind-fulness meditation" or "just sitting." Contrary to popular beliefs about meditation, this approach to mindfulness is not about obtaining enlightenment or entering a trance or altered state. The purpose is not to clear the mind or to experience anything in particular. Rather, mindfulness meditation is about simply sitting quietly and observing your experience in the present moment. It is about looking *at* your thoughts and feelings instead of experiencing the world *through* your thoughts and feelings. Far from clearing your mind, you are likely to observe quite a lot going on there. This is natural. Thinking is what the mind does— all the time. Mindfulness does not interrupt or change this. Being mindful means simply observing that process in a defused and accepting way, with compassion. It means being aware of ourselves as the context and of our thoughts and feelings, as well as everything else we are experiencing, as the content.

Make the time.   Ten minutes every day is a good place to start. Once this becomes a regular part of your routine, you can try slowly expand-ing this time to thirty minutes. If you are like most Americans, you regularly devote this much time to a reasonably good sitcom. If you are worried about losing track of the time, set a timer.

Find a quiet place.   While it's best to practice in a place where there is not a lot of activity, it's not necessary to eliminate all distractions. When practicing mindfulness, occasional distractions are simply part of the content of your experience, to be noted and accepted before returning your focus to your breathing, your thoughts, and the rest of your experience in the moment.

Sit comfortably, but not too comfortably.   Most people who practice mindfulness meditation on a regular basis recommend sitting on the floor, usually with the legs crossed. It is important to maintain an alert, erect posture while you are sitting, and many people find this easier to do while sitting on the floor. If this is uncomfortable, a chair works just as well, as long as it is not a chair that encourages slouching. The best posture is one in which you are reasonably comfortable but can remain alert. While mindfulness meditation can be relaxing, relaxation is not the purpose of mindfulness. Most importantly, you do not want to be so comfortable that you fall asleep. Lay your hands in your lap so that your arms are supported, and remember to sit up straight.

Start with a body scan.   If you find that you are distracted by tickles and itches or tension in your body, it can help to begin with a quick body scan (exercise 7.9), noticing whatever you are aware of in your body, acknowledging that experience, accepting or making room for it, and moving on. With practice, this can be done in less than sixty seconds.

Watch your breathing.   A good way to bring your focus to the present moment is to observe your breathing as described in exercise 7.11. Simply focus on the one spot where you are most aware of the air as it enters and leaves your body. Allow your attention to rest on this spot, observing your breath as it comes and goes. When your mind wanders to other things, notice and accept that this has happened, and then gently bring your attention back to your breathing.

Listen to your heartbeat.   As things get quieter, you might shift your attention to the soft, pulsating sensation of your heart beating. Some people prefer to observe the breath while others prefer to observe their heartbeat. Focus on whichever sensation you find easiest to attend to.

Notice your thoughts.   As you sit, you will begin to notice your thoughts. Being mindful means noticing these thoughts in a defused way. In other words, watching your thoughts flow past from the banks of the river rather than jumping into the river and being carried away by the thoughts. Continuing to be aware of your breathing or your heartbeat while simultaneously observing your thoughts can help you to stay grounded in the present moment, separate from your thoughts. When you notice that you have been carried away by a stream of thinking, notice this, then gently bring your focus back to your breath or your heartbeat as a way of reconnecting with your experience in the present moment.

Notice thoughts that are judgments.   Expect to have thoughts that judge and criticize your performance. Since this is all about your experience, there is no right or wrong way to practice mindfulness. Even so, you will likely notice thoughts like "Am I doing this right?" or "What's supposed to be happening here?" Observe these thoughts as thoughts, accept that they are there as part of your experience, and bring your focus back to your breathing or heartbeat.

Notice your feelings.   Allow your awareness to include the emotions that you are feeling. Notice that it is possible to feel and experience those emotions fully, being mindful of them as part of your experience. Since the emotions are part of your experience, you are bigger than the emotions. If you notice yourself struggling with your feelings or otherwise engaging with them down on the "content level," notice this. Then practice letting go of control, accepting and keeping your hands off of the emotions. Allow the feelings to be there along with every other aspect of your experience, leaning into the emotions.

Practicing mindfulness in this way will help you to develop all of the skills presented so far when you apply the LLAMP approach to worry. By becoming a more skilled observer of your own thinking process, you will be better able to apply the labeling step, identifying thoughts that are worries and the anxiety that accompanies them. Mindful sitting is a way of being that does not engage the control response and will therefore help you to become more comfortable with the step of letting go of control. Practicing mindfulness also means practicing acceptance of your thoughts and feelings by experiencing them in a defused way (as separate from your self and from what they refer to). Mindfulness of the present moment can improve your ability to experience all that the present has to offer and help you to be less judgmental of yourself and others. Practicing mindful sitting on a regular basis can also help you to become more objective about your experiences and reduce the problems that can accompany being carried away by your emotions.

Mindful Walking

Another way to integrate mindfulness into your daily life is to practice mindfulness while taking a walk. There are many forms of walking meditation. Some of them start with a focus on the actual act of walking, and others encourage mindful observation of the environment. All forms of walking meditation, however, involve observation and acceptance of the thoughts and feelings that arise while walking.

Walk slowly in a circle. This way, you are less likely to be distracted by going somewhere specific. You can do this in your backyard or in your living room. Close your eyes for a few steps, focusing on the soles of your feet. Observe the sensations of each foot as it first makes contact with the ground or floor. Notice when it leaves the floor. As you walk, observe the movements of the process we call walking. Notice other sensations in your body that arise as you continue to walk. Observe the thoughts that enter and leave your mind as you are walking. What other aspects of your experience are there? Are you making judgments about the exercise? Are you feeling any emotions?

Take a walk in nature.   Going for a longer walk outdoors provides more stimulation and objects in the environment to observe. As you are walking, look at the trees, the sky, the ground. Notice thoughts that come to mind when you see all of these elements of your environment. Try to simply observe and notice without judging or evaluating. It may help to label what you are seeing by quietly saying the name of each item that you observe. As you look at the tree, say "tree." Notice that once the word is gone, the object you are looking at remains, continuing to exist in the silence. Observe that the word is just a thought produced by your mind, separate from the object.

Take a walk in a town or city.   Urban or suburban environments offer an abundance of man-made elements for mindful observation. As you walk in these settings, allow yourself to notice features of architecture and design. Be mindful of the lines and shapes that you are observing. Notice the differing textures of the materials that objects are made of. Notice similarities in line, shape, and texture that can be found in buildings, furniture, and clothing. If you notice your mind producing categories like "classical" or "modern" or judgments like "pretty" or "ugly," observe that these are simply labels produced by your mind, letting them go and bringing your focus back to the experience itself, separate from the language used to talk about it. Notice that categories like "buildings," "furniture," and "clothing" are also products of your mind, and allow yourself to observe objects as they are, focusing on their shapes, sizes, and textures.

Focus on color.   As you are walking, shift your focus to the colors that you see. Take your time, looking at the world to see what colors are there. It may help to label the color you are looking at. Say "yellow" to yourself, and really see the color yellow. Notice that once the word has been said, the experience of the color continues. "Yellow" is just a word, but the experience that you call "yellow" is happening to you right now. Look for other colors that catch your eye, and experience the color without attending to the objects involved.

As a variation on this, pick a specific color before you start your walk, for example, blue. As you are walking, look specifically for the color blue. When you see the color blue, simply observe and experience that color. Stay with one sample of the color blue for several moments, drinking in the experience of the color, then move on, looking for more blue. Allow yourself to fully experience and enjoy all of the blue that your environment has to offer.

Mindful Eating

You have already had some experience with mindful eating in completing exercises 7.5 and 7.6. Since eating involves all five of the senses, it is an excellent opportunity to practice mindfulness every day. The visual appearance, scent, taste, texture, and even the sound of food are all elements of experience that can ground us in the here and now. In addition to developing your ability to connect to the present moment, mindful eating has the added benefit of helping to increase your awareness of hunger and satiation sensations, which can reduce tendencies toward overeating. Perhaps the easiest time to practice mindful eating is when eating alone. However, it is possible to be mindful of shared dining experiences as well.

Be mindful before the meal.   An effective way to warm up before mindful eating is to attend to sensations of hunger before the meal even begins. Notice your thoughts as well as bodily sensations that you are aware of before the food is in sight. If you are at work, you can start by being mindful of food-related thoughts and hunger before leaving for lunch. If you are preparing the meal yourself, you can use the opportunity to practice some mindful cooking, going through the motions of meal preparation very slowly. Notice the thoughts and emotions that you experience in anticipation of and immediately before beginning a meal.

Look at your food.   Professional as well as amateur chefs are aware of the importance of presentation when preparing a meal. Advertisers are acutely aware of the importance of food's visual impact and spend millions of dollars to make food look appealing. Even when there has been no effort expended on presentation, the visual appearance of food enhances our experience of it. Before you bite into that apple, look at the colors in its skin. If it's a potato chip, consider the texture of its surface and its golden color.

Smell. This is something that most of us learn to do as part of enjoying a meal. When eating mindfully, allow yourself extra time to savor food's aroma. You might find that you are more likely to do this when you're eating food that is warm, but cold foods offer a variety of scents as well. Smell the fruit, bread, or nuts that you are about to eat. Before taking the first sip of your beverage, allow yourself a long, slow sniff. Even as you are chewing, notice how the smell of the food accentuates your taste experience.

Notice the texture. Before you even take the first bite, it is possible to notice food's texture. For example, notice how it feels to cut your meat. Tear off a piece of bread slowly, noticing how it separates. When you bite into your food, do so slowly, noticing the resistance of the different textures. How is biting into an egg roll different from biting into mashed potatoes? Hold each bite in your mouth momentarily before beginning to chew. Feel the texture of the food on your tongue. What does the food feel like as you are chewing?

Listen to your food. Different foods make different sounds. Dishes that are served hot often sizzle temptingly. When you bite into crackers, apples, fried foods, breads, nuts, cereals, chips, and popcorn you are greeted by distinctive sounds. These sounds continue as you chew. Close your eyes and listen to the sounds that your food makes.

Taste. Many people find that when they eat a meal on the run, they are seldom aware of the taste of the food after the first bite or so. Mindful eating means staying focused on how each bite of food tastes, focusing again and again on *this* bite, *this* moment. When you first place the food in your mouth, you are aware of its texture and temperature first. Take a moment before chewing to become aware of how the food tastes. As you begin to chew slowly, notice how the taste changes. Do you taste the food more on the front of your tongue or on the back? Notice how much you salivate in response to the taste. Also, notice the judgments you will invariably have about the taste. Simply observe these, without getting caught up in them. This is not about being a food critic, it's about tasting. Swallow. Wait a moment. Watch for and notice the aftertaste of the food you are eating. How long does it take for the taste to begin to fade after the food has left your mouth?

Observe your thoughts. As in the other mindfulness exercises you've tried, pay attention to the thoughts that come to mind as you are eating. Observe your thoughts without being carried away by them. Use your mindfulness of the food and the process of eating to help you stay anchored in the present moment, observing your thoughts as one of many aspects of the present moment along with the bite of food that you are currently eating.

Feel your feelings. Notice the emotions you experience while eating mindfully. If you're having a difficult day and experiencing anxiety or sadness, this is still a fine time to practice mindful eating. Rather than using the food to distract yourself from what you are feeling, eating mindfully simply means being fully present to both the food you are eating *and* the feelings you are feeling. Slow down and experience both the smells, textures, and tastes as well as the emotions that are there for you in the present moment. Notice that there is room for all of these aspects of your experience. Your experience of the food, your thoughts, and your emotions are all content. You are the context.

MINDFULNESS & THE LLAMP APPROACH

At this point, you should have a more detailed understanding of what is meant by each of the first four steps of the LLAMP approach. The exercises presented in the last four chapters will help you to develop the skills and understand the concepts involved in applying each of these steps. Now is a good time to begin using all of the first four steps together when you become aware of worry and anxiety. Here's how the steps of labeling, letting go, acceptance, and mindfulness work together and can be applied as a unified approach to worry when it occurs.

I. *Label:* By labeling specific thought content as "worry," "rumination," or whatever helps you to identify these thoughts as nonproductive and not helpful, you will know that now is a good time to apply the LLAMP approach. Labeling your thoughts as nonproductive will also help you begin to step back from them, since in labeling your thoughts, you are looking at the thoughts rather than through them.

2.   *Let go:* As soon as you identify and label the worry-related thoughts, remind yourself to let go of the desire to control or get rid of these thoughts. This second step may seem counterintuitive. You might think, "Well, if the thoughts are nonproductive, shouldn't I get rid of them?" Remember that when it comes to inside experiences like thoughts and feelings, trying to get rid of them is part of the problem. You can label a thought as nonproductive and still be willing to have it be there, and in fact, that is the whole point of this approach. Taking a deep breath and relaxing your muscles will help you to "let go of the rope" that is your struggle to control your thoughts and feelings. Don't worry about being 100 percent successful with this step. Its purpose is to momentarily interrupt the automatic control response, allowing room for the next step.

3.   *Accept:* In the LLAMP approach, acceptance means observing your thoughts and feelings in a defused way. Applying this step is like panning back with a camera to get a panoramic perspective. You are reminding yourself that these thoughts and feelings are the content, and you are the context. Saying things like "I am having the thought that ..." can help you to achieve this distance and experience your thoughts and feelings as separate from your self. If you notice that you are pulled back into a content-level struggle with your thoughts and feelings, go back to step number two for a moment, reminding yourself to let go of control, and then pan back to the experience of yourself as context and your thoughts as content. Observe your thoughts in a defused way, as separate from their referents.

4.   *Mindfulness:* Once you have shifted to the observer perspective, you are in a position to begin to attend to other aspects of your experience of the present moment. Applying mindfulness here is not a way to distract yourself, but rather a way to support acceptance and maintain the context/observer perspective. Continue to observe your thoughts and feelings, but allow yourself to also be aware of where you are and what you're doing in

the present moment. Allow yourself to notice sounds, sights, scents, and other sensations. If you like, do a quick body scan or spend a moment observing your breathing. Make room for all of your experience, your thoughts and feelings included.

Using these four steps together is a very fluid process. You may find yourself going back and forth between the steps or applying two of them simultaneously. This is fine—the sequence presented here is only intended to provide a structure for the application of these principles. You may find it necessary to spend more time on one step than on another or to repeat a step over and over again. This is something you will have to get a feel for, developing your own unique style.

You will have the opportunity to practice applying all of these steps together in chapter 9 when you develop your own individualized program of exposure. First, however, to help you determine what specific type of exposure will be most helpful for you and why, we will move on to the final step of the LLAMP approach: proceeding in the right direction.

CHAPTER EIGHT

PROCEED IN THE RIGHT DIRECTION

The purpose of applying the LLAMP approach to worry and anxiety is to develop willingness. As we have seen, willingness on the inside means a willingness to think, feel, and experience all of your thoughts, feelings, and sensations. This is the acceptance part of acceptance and commitment therapy, embodied in the first four steps: labeling, letting go, acceptance, and mindfulness. Willingness on the *outside* means willingness to take action. This is "proceeding in the right direction," the commitment part of ACT, and the final step of the LLAMP approach.

Proceeding in the right direction involves choosing a direction, committing to specific actions, and following through with those actions, even as we think, feel, and experience all that goes along with that. Since the direction that we choose is guided by our values, this chapter focuses on clarifying what it is that you value most in life and making an honest assessment of whether your actions are consistent with those values. People who engage in frequent worry often respond to anxiety with avoidance and procrastination. They may believe that it is impossible to take action until they have resolved all of their reservations and doubts. Proceeding in the right direction is about taking action even as we experience reservations and doubts.

When our actions are guided by a desire to control or avoid feelings like anxiety, we often experience them as automatic rather than chosen. Instead of acting, we are reacting. These automatic actions are often inconsistent with what we truly value. For example, the overweight man who values being healthy and fit worries about not finding time to exercise and reaches for another slice of pizza. Proceeding in the right direction means replacing these automatic reactions with intentional, reasoned actions that are guided by our values rather than by avoidance. You can probably think of several ways that you automatically react to anxiety that actually move you in the wrong direction, away from what is truly important to you. Procrastination, social isolation, and use of alcohol or other drugs are just a few common examples. Even the act of worrying itself can be an automatic reaction to anxiety that moves us away from taking valued action.

CARING VS. WORRYING

As mentioned in chapter 1, worriers often believe that the act of worrying will increase the likelihood of a favorable outcome. In this way, worry serves as a substitute for action. When we worry about someone or something, we often see it as evidence that we care about the focus of our worry. For example, a mother who worries about her adult son and expresses this by calling him several times a day might say to him, "I only call because I care about you." The question is, are the calls an expression of caring or an expression of worry? Are these the same thing?

Is Worrying the Same as Caring?

Worrying is an attempt to exert control over the future by thinking about it. In this way, worry is something that occurs on the inside, and its effects on the outside world are only imaginary. Worry behaviors (like the worried mother's calls to her son) occur on the outside but are still focused on decreasing anxiety and discomfort inside the worrier. This is very different from caring. When we are caring for someone or something, we do the things that support or advance the best interests of the person or thing that we care about. Caring has an impact on the outside, and it may or may not reduce our own anxiety.

Consider the difference between worrying about your houseplants and caring for your houseplants. If you are away from home for a week, you can worry about your houseplants every single day and still return home to find them brown and wilted. Worrying is not watering. Similarly, the mother who calls her son several times a day, even when her constant calls interfere with his ability to get things done at work and cause friction in his marriage, is worrying about her son but is failing to care for him as well as she might.

If you apply this distinction to yourself and the areas of your own life that you worry about, the question to ask is, "Would I rather worry about my life or care about and care for it?" Do you ever confuse worrying about some aspect of your life with caring for it? To answer this question, it helps to get clear about what worry looks like and what caring looks like for each area of concern. Let's consider concern for the environment. The following table looks at the difference between worrying about the environment and caring about it. Which list of responses is likely to have a greater impact on the environment?

TABLE 8.1	
Worrying about the *environment* involves …	Caring about the *environment* involves …
• Having your drinking water tested • Reading data on air/water quality • Thinking about the plight of future generations • Wearing a protective face mask	• Driving a low-emissions vehicle • Recycling bottles and cans • Using mass transit • Volunteering for clean-up projects • Buying from eco-friendly producers

EXERCISE 8.1: Caring About vs. Worrying About Your Life

In the tables below, list responses that would express worrying and those that would demonstrate caring in these different areas of your life.

Worrying about your *health* involves ...	Caring about your *health* involves ...

Worrying about your *finances* involves ...	Caring about your *finances* involves ...

Worrying about your *relationships* involves ...	Caring about your *relationships* involves ...

Worrying about your *career* involves ...	Caring about your *career* involves ...

As you look at the list of responses that demonstrate caring, notice that many of these are actions that you can take. Caring, as opposed to worrying, is about taking action. Understanding what it is that you value in life is the first step toward caring in an active way.

VALUES: WHAT DO YOU CARE ABOUT?

Although it may not be difficult to identify the general areas of your life that you care about (health, relationships, finances, or career), it may take a bit more thought to specify what is most important to you within each of these domains. For example, when it comes to relationships, do you care more about some relationships in your life than you do about others? Is it more important to spend time with someone you can talk to, or is it more important that the two of you enjoy the same activities? When you consider your career, how important is the size of your paycheck relative to how much you enjoy your work? What quality do you value most in whatever work you do? Is it autonomy? Creativity? Lack of stress or effort? One purpose of this chapter is to help you identify your own answers to questions like these.

What Are Values?

When we use the word "values" we are referring to those qualities and experiences that add value to your life. Clarifying your values, therefore, means deciding what is important to you and warrants the most investment of your limited time, energy, and resources. Being clear about your values is especially important when two valued areas of your life are in conflict with one another. For example, when you are faced with the common choice of working longer hours for more pay or having more free time and less money, clarity about your values can provide important direction. In addition to guiding your choices and actions, a clear sense of your values can also provide an increased sense of meaning in your life.

Values are not morals.   For many people, the word "values" brings up thoughts about morality and rules for living a good life. As it's used here and in the context of acceptance and commitment therapy, the word values does not refer to any set of rules or code of conduct imposed from without. On the contrary, your values are your own and are highly personal. Rather than being imposed from the outside, values are internal. Instead of guiding our actions like an external list of rules, values guide our choices from the inside, like an internal compass.

Values cannot be evaluated. Your values are your values—they are neither good nor bad. You can compare your values to someone else's and find that they are different. But if you try to evaluate values and determine which ones are best, you run into a problem. What do you use to evaluate something? You judge and evaluate the value of something using your values. If you are going to evaluate your values, whose values will you use to do that? The only choice you have, if you are doing the evaluating, is to use your own. If someone were to ask you "Why do you value that?" the only answer you could give would be to refer to another value. The next reasonable question would be "Well, why do you value *that?*" You value what you value, and that, in a very unique way, is that. Values are one aspect of yourself that you cannot judge to be inadequate. Here's why: Suppose you looked at a list of your values and were aware that there was something missing from them that, in your opinion, made them inadequate. Why would the lack of this something make your values inadequate? Well, because that something has value. But how do you know that? If you are aware that something that is missing from your values is of value, that means that you are aware of the value of that something, which means it isn't missing from your values after all! In this way, your values, by definition, are beyond judgment. They're perfect. The only question is, are you allowing them to be your guide?

Values are not feelings. People often confuse the question of what they value with how they feel about someone or something. The problem with this is that feelings, being on the inside, are beyond our control and tend to come and go. For example, consider your feelings about the work that you do. Do you always feel the same way about your job? Applying yourself diligently only on days when you have feelings of liking your job and completely blowing off work on those days when you are not loving your job is probably not going to advance your career. This is where commitment comes in. If your response to difficult emotions is to abandon movement in a valued direction, you will never get anywhere that you want to go. The same is true whether you're pursuing a marriage, an exercise routine, a healthy diet, or writing a book. Commitment, or proceeding in the right direction, is the expression of values as action, on the outside, independent of what you may be feeling on the inside. In this way, values allow us to coordinate and direct our actions over the long term.

Values are not goals. While a value can point you in a particular direction, and values often suggest specific goals, values and goals are not the same thing. This distinction is important because sometimes we may do things in the service of a goal that actually move us away from a valued direction. Think about the executive who values taking good care of his family. In service of this value, he has the goal of making good money. If his focus on the goal of making money leads him to work sixty-plus hours per week, getting home exhausted after his children are asleep, he may be losing sight of the value that inspired his goal. People who pursue the same goal can do so because of different values. Consider several politicians running for the same office. They all share the common goal of getting elected, but does this mean they have the same values? One of them might have selected this goal based on the values of public service and making the world a better place. Does it follow that anyone pursuing the goal of election to public office shares these values?

When we mistake goals for values, we risk losing sight of our values and of the direction they have to offer. Consider the single person who says that she values being married. Being married is a goal, not a value. A goal (like "being married") is something you can get or not get. A value is something that you already have, that you can choose to listen to or not to listen to. To clear up the confusion between values and goals, it can be helpful to ask "What would the benefits be of obtaining this goal?" The answer to this question will often reveal the value hiding behind the goal. For example, for the goal of being married, the benefits might include shared experiences, intimacy, and love. These are values. Getting married is a goal in service of these values. Even if this goal is not met, the values pointing in that direction remain and may point to other goals that lie in the same direction. More importantly, if the goal of marriage provides the direction rather than the values behind it, it is possible to end up married but without shared experiences, intimacy, or love.

Another problem arises when we focus too much on goals and lose sight of the values behind them. When the direction in our lives is guided by a goal rather than a value, what happens when we have successfully obtained that goal? If the goal is the only thing driving our progress, achieving the goal means that progress stops. Many people experience a loss of life direction after reaching a major goal, accompanied by feelings of depression and disorientation. Being mindful of the values that prompted you to set the goal can give you a sense of continuing progress and clarity about what comes next. Unlike goals, values are directions, not destinations.

Clarifying Your Values

While you may have spent considerable time contemplating your goals and perhaps worrying about which goals to set, you may not have spent much time thinking about your values. One way to begin looking at what it is that adds value to your life is to consider the range of experiences that you have had or would like to have in your life.

EXERCISE 8.2: Valued Experiences

For this exercise you will need a pen and fifteen three-by-five-inch index cards.

1. On each card, write down a few words describing an experience that you value. These may include experiences that you have often, ones that you've had only once, or that you would like to have in the future. The experiences can include accomplishing something worthwhile, time spent with someone special, or time spent alone. The descriptions on each card should look something like this:

    "Eating ice cream in my pajamas while watching old movies"

    "Going to Paris someday"

    "Working out and being healthy"

    "Adding a deck to my house"

    "Riding bikes with John"

2. Spread the cards out face up, so that you can see what you have written on them. Consider what a life filled with all of these experiences would be like.

3. Imagine that you will be forced to give up one of these experiences. Either through illness, financial losses, or

just a series of circumstances beyond your control, one of these experiences will never happen again. Considering all of your cards, choose the one experience that you are most willing to give up and have erased from your life. Place this card to the side. Imagine what your life would be like without this experience.

4. Repeat this step, selecting the next experience that you would be willing to lose forever from your life. Place that card on top of the first one that you set aside. Repeat this process until you have only five cards left. Each time you remove a card, look at the cards that remain and try to imagine a life limited to these experiences.

5. When you have five cards remaining, look at these five valued experiences. What do they have in common? Are there people involved in these experiences? Who? Are you alone for many of them? Where are you for most of these experiences? What types of things are you doing? Does it cost a lot of money to do these things?

6. What do these experiences tell you about what you value most in life? Make a list of the values reflected in these experiences. This will be a working list of your core values. Describe each value with a brief statement that captures what it is about these experiences that is of value to you. Keep this list. You will be adding to it and using it in subsequent exercises.

Another way to think about your personal values is to consider what is most important to you within several different areas or domains of your life. In the following exercise, you will be encouraged to consider several areas of your life, like family, career, and spirituality, and what experiences or qualities are most important to you within each of these areas.

EXERCISE 8.3:
Shopping at the Values Mall

You are going shopping at the Values Mall. All of the experiences or qualities that you buy will be part of your life. Those that you do not buy will be absent from your life. There are seven stores in the mall. In a given store, you can buy as many items as you like or none at all. However, you have exactly $100 to spend. On a separate sheet of paper, copy each value that you want to have in your life along with the cost of that value. Keep a running total of how much you have spent, and do not go over $100. Since the costs of moving in a valued direction vary based on individual circumstances, all of the prices in the Values Mall have been randomly assigned. Happy shopping!

WELCOME TO THE VALUES MALL!

Leisure and Learning Lane

Traveling	$6
Learning new things	$8
Relaxation and meditation	$7
Enjoying a hobby or sport	$5
Enjoying art, music, or literature	$6

The Family and Friends Store

Helping loved ones in need	$9
Hanging out and laughing with loved ones	$8
Emotional intimacy and personal sharing	$6
Meeting new people	$7
Belonging to a club or group	$5

The Love Boutique

Long-term commitment and fidelity	$8
Companionship and shared interests	$5
Physical intimacy and sex	$7
Romance and excitement	$8
Emotional connection with partner	$9

Career Mart

Making a lot of money	$8
Doing work that is challenging or creative	$7
Helping others	$8
Flexibility and autonomy	$5
Doing something easy and low-stress	$9

The Spirituality Shop

Prayer and meditation	$7
Knowledge/understanding of spiritual writings	$7
Believing and practicing a specific religion	$9
Belonging to a spiritual community	$5
Feeling connected to a higher power	$6

Community Corner

Being politically aware and involved	$8
Volunteering to help others	$6
Protecting the environment	$6

Patriotism $8

Being ethical and fair $7

The Mind-Body Connection

Eating healthy foods $7

Exercising regularly $9

Psychological awareness/mental health $6

Managing stress well $7

Living as long as possible $6

Thank you for shopping at the Values Mall. Was it easy to decide what to buy and what to leave behind? Did you have to make some difficult choices? In which stores did you make the most purchases? Where did you make the fewest purchases? Look at the items that you bought and the stores or categories where you made the most purchases. What are the values reflected in your choices? Add these to the list of core values that you developed in exercise 8.2.

═══

Before moving on to the next section, take a careful look at your list of core values. Are there other experiences or qualities that are important for adding value to your life? If you can think of any additional values that are as important as those already listed, add them to the list. Try to limit yourself to ten statements or less. You may find that several of your value statements overlap and can be combined into one broader statement. Look at each item, and make sure that you are not listing actions or goals. For example, if you listed "Go skiing with friends," this is an action or goal, not a value. To get at the value that lies behind the goal or action, ask yourself, "What would the benefits be of taking this action or obtaining this goal?" A given goal can reveal any of a number of different values. For example, the value behind the goal "Go skiing with friends" could be "Spending fun times with loved ones," "Exercise and physical fitness," or "Learning new things."

CARING: VALUES & RESPONSE-ABILITY

Remember that, as illustrated in exercise 8.1, caring involves taking action. When you make the move from worrying to caring, you are acknowledging responsibility for your values. The word "responsibility" has negative connotations for many people, evoking memories of lecturing authority figures and feelings of guilt. Steven Hayes and his colleagues (1999) have pointed out that the word "responsible" was originally two words: "response" and "able." When we acknowledge response-ability for our values, we are acknowledging that we are indeed *able* to *respond* in ways that put our values into action. If you have a value, and you are response-able, this means that it is up to you to do something about whatever it is that you value. This is a frightening thought for many people, but it is a liberating one as well. When you avoid response-ability, you are in effect saying that you are not able to respond and that you have no choices. Response-ability means that you actually can choose to take a different course and end up with a different outcome.

Let's consider what happens with a core value like concern for the environment when you begin to take responsibility for it. Often when we think of things that we value, we say things like "It's important." Thus, in talking about preserving the environment, you might say something like "Air quality is important." Suppose you made this comment to your congressman. Now suppose he responded by saying, "I disagree. Air quality is *not* important." How would you prove him wrong? You might argue that poor air quality ultimately leads to global warming. What would you say, then, when the lawmaker countered with "Global warming is not important." Well, you might go on to explain that global warming is indeed important because it affects the quality of life for future generations. Now suppose that this member of congress were to say, "Future generations are not important. I'll be retired before they're old enough to vote." How could you argue with that? Essentially, what this elected leader is saying is that air quality, global warming, and future generations are not important to *him*. The problem with saying "It's important" when thinking about our values is that we often leave it at that. We assume that if it's important, then someone (lawmakers, corporations, the public)—that is, someone other than *us*—will do something about it. When we take response-ability for our values, however, we are acknowledging that the importance or nonimportance of anything lies not out there, but within us. We have the ability to do something about it. We are response-able. Caring about the environment (or anything else) always means taking some sort of action.

EXERCISE 8.4: Acknowledge Response-ability

1. Look at your list of core values. For each of these values, consider the following question: What have you done in the past week that demonstrates a commitment to this value? It may be something very simple or very small, but try to think of some action that you have taken that is consistent with each value on the list. If you have not taken any action in the past week, how about the past month? The past year?

2. In general, how would you rate your performance when it comes to taking actions that are consistent with each of your core values? Consider the range of possible actions that you could take in the service of each value and rate the actions you have taken as a percentage of what is reasonably possible. For example, if you are doing all that you reasonably can, you can rate your actions as 100 percent. If you have done nothing at all in spite of obvious opportunities for action, your rating may be closer to 0 percent. Be sure to give yourself credit for even small actions, but rate these relative to all possible actions that you consider to be reasonable.

GOALS

Earlier, we discussed the importance of distinguishing between values and goals. Reaching a specific goal is just one of many possible steps in a valued direction. Your goals may change over time, even as your values stay the same. As mentioned above, sometimes people become so focused on a goal that they lose sight of the values behind the goal. This can lead to moves in the wrong direction or a loss of direction after obtaining a specific goal. While it is important to avoid focusing on goals to the exclusion of remembering your values, goals are still necessary if you are to make progress in a valued direction.

Setting a goal means specifying a target outcome and committing to a process that moves us toward that outcome. Notice that goal setting involves not only an outcome, but a process. A process is a series of actions. When we commit to a goal, we are not committing to the outcome (which is impossible to guarantee), but to a series of actions that will move us in the direction of the desired outcome.

Staying on Track

If values are like an internal compass pointing us in the right direction, setting goals is like establishing route markers along a path that moves us in that direction. Goals keep us on track. This is helpful for a number of reasons. For one, setting and moving toward goals gives us a sense of progress and movement that we might not otherwise have. Goals channel and focus our activities in ways that move us further in valued directions than do more random, diffuse actions. For example, suppose you have a core value of doing something creative. You might manifest this value in flurries of activity, spending a little time drawing one day, toying with an idea for a sculpture on another day, or watching a television program about flower arrangement the next. In some cases, especially if you value exploring and trying as many new things as possible, engaging in this range of activities might be a goal in itself. In other cases, when the value is to create something, these sporadic actions may be less than satisfying. By setting specific goals, these actions can be channeled in ways that offer more of a sense of movement toward the value of doing something creative. Examples of goals in this area would be "drawing a portrait of my cat," "completing a sculpture for my yard," or "making a flower arrangement for my home." Realistic, obtainable goals provide us with feedback that we are indeed progressing in the valued direction.

This feedback is especially important because the paths we follow are not always straight. Sometimes it's hard to tell if we are indeed proceeding in the right direction. If you have ever hiked up a mountain path, you know that while your intention is to move upward, toward the summit, it is usually necessary to move to the left and to the right in order to do so. We find these switchbacks in life all the time. For example, you may value autonomy and independence in your working life. To have this autonomy, however, it may be helpful to have a degree, a license, or a certification in your area of expertise. Proceeding toward this goal will likely involve participation in a very structured certification process in which your work is closely supervised. Initially, this may feel like movement away from your valued direction of increased autonomy and independence. If you are not clear about how the goal of certification lines up with your value of autonomy, you might become impatient with the requirements and withdraw from the certification process. The result may be fewer opportunities for independence in the future. Recognizing the structure and constraint of the credentialing process as a necessary switchback that ultimately moves you further along in the valued direction of autonomy can help you to maintain your commitment.

Setting Goals

When setting goals, take one core value at a time. You might want to start with a value that you feel is not manifested in your life at this time. Start with an area where you feel stuck. Look at this core value and ask yourself, "What would make this value real in my life?" Try to think of something practical and obtainable. Make sure that the goal is within the realm of what is possible, given your current life situation. For example, if you are over fifty, out of shape, and lacking in a science or engineering background, the goal of becoming an astronaut is probably not obtainable. Joining a hiking group, reading books about outer space, or volunteering at the planetarium move you in the same direction as the astronaut goal, but these options have the added advantage of being possible. Although it is important to be realistic, don't let this stop you from being bold. Setting impossible goals won't help you, but setting difficult or challenging goals is fine. Remember, this is about living a life that you value. The stakes are your values and your life. So don't skimp!

When you set a goal that is challenging or that lies some distance in the future, it is usually helpful to set a number of subgoals that are more short term. Short-term goals will indicate your progress from where you are now as you move toward the long-term goal. These are the route markers that will keep you on track. When we consider a long-term goal, it can often seem so large or complex that we don't know how to begin to move toward it. Short-term goals lie near enough in the future to suggest immediate action.

Barriers to Setting Goals

People who tend to worry a lot often have trouble setting goals. Common worries related to goal setting include fears of committing to one option at the cost of others, fear of choosing the wrong goal, and fear of failing once the goal is selected. Many people respond to these worries by avoiding goal setting altogether.

Fear of committing.   Inherent in the action of choosing an option is the loss of other options. Choosing to commit to a goal often means losing a sense of freedom and control that comes with having other options available. Selecting one option means letting go of the others, at least for the time being. The security of keeping all of your options open, however, comes at a cost. Very often, the worst choice you can make is not choosing.

Choosing and committing to a goal can be like standing in a hallway lined with doors. While all of the doors may be open to you, and they may even be clearly labeled, you cannot know what it is really like on the other side of a given door until you pass through it. As long as you are standing in the hallway, you have a sense of being in control because you're free to go through whichever door you choose. If you pass through any one of the doors, however, there is no guarantee that all of the other doors will still be open should you return to the hallway later. This fear of losing options may lead you to remain in the hall, carefully keeping all of the doors open. The problem with this, of course, is that you may end up spending all of your life in the hallway. Keeping your options open means never going through a door, and never getting what's on the other side. You get to keep all of your options but that's all that you get. It's like going to a restaurant and reading the menu but never ordering anything. It's nice to see that you have all those choices, but if you don't order, you're going to leave just as hungry as you were when you walked in.

Fear of choosing the wrong goal. You may recall that the single trait that most worriers share is a low tolerance for uncertainty. Often, people who have trouble selecting a goal want to know the outcome of choosing a particular goal before they commit to it. In many cases this involves not only a fear of a negative outcome but fear of the possibility of a potentially better outcome. In other words, the fear is often not so much about making a bad choice as not making the "best" choice. The problem with this line of thinking is that the best choice may not be the best until we choose it. As long as a goal is something we are thinking about but haven't committed to, it's easy to think of it as being better or worse than another goal. When it comes to the eventual outcome, often these ideas about the relative value of a prospective goal are not as important as our ability to commit to whichever goal we choose. Once you commit to a goal, it is your job to embrace that choice and to *make* that choice the best one. As a theoretical construct, the best choice does not already exist out there independent of your choosing and committing to it.

Fear of failure. When you consider committing to a specific goal, especially one that is challenging or risky, you may find that one of the first questions to arise is "What if I don't succeed?" Nobody enjoys failure, and a certain degree of anxiety when faced with this possibility is natural and unavoidable. However, failure—which is always a possible outcome—need not be a barrier to commitment. It is important to remember that setting a goal involves both specifying a targeted outcome and a process (a series of actions) that moves you toward that outcome. When you commit to a goal, you are not committing to an outcome (which is impossible to guarantee), but to a process. This commitment to a series of actions that move us in the direction of the desired outcome is especially important when we fail to obtain a goal. It's the commitment to the process that allows us to pick up the pieces and carry on or proceed in the right direction.

EXERCISE 8.5: Making a Value Map

1. In this exercise and the ones that follow, you will be creating a series of Value Maps, writing about your values

and goals using the format on the following page. Start by looking at your list of core values. Select an important core value that you would like to work on moving toward. Copy this value on the blank line at the top of the page next to "Value:".

2. Think of one long-term goal that would indicate significant movement in the direction of this value. What would make this value real in your life? Make sure that the goal is obtainable and realistic, but don't be afraid of being bold. Write out the goal under the heading "Long-Term Goal."

3. Now think of several short-term goals that would indicate a progression from where you are now to this long-term goal. Remember, short-term goals should lie near enough in the future to suggest immediate action. List these goals under the heading "Short-Term Goals."

4. Repeat this exercise for several other core values, starting with a fresh Value Map for each value. Focus on those values where you gave yourself a low rating in the previous exercise. These are valued directions where you have noticed a lack of committed action. (You will be completing the remaining sections of the Value Map in the exercises that follow.)

A Value Map

Value: _____

_____

Long-Term Goal: _____

_____

Short-Term Goals: _____

_____

_____

_____

_____

_____

Time/Place: _____

Actions: _____

_____

_____

_____

_____

Barriers: _____

_____

_____

_____

_____

_____

TAKING ACTION

Setting a goal is a commitment to a process that moves you in a valued direction. A process is a series of actions. Actions are where the rubber meets the road in living a life consistent with your values. Having set long-term goals that are in line with your values and having broken the journey into a series of short-term goals, what comes next? What can you do this week to move toward one of your short-term goals? As you consider this, you may become aware of worries, doubts, reservations, fears, and a wide range of other thoughts and feelings. Notice all of these as potential barriers to taking action, and remember that being willing to act means being willing to think, feel, and experience all that comes up as you proceed with the action. We will take a closer look at these potential barriers in a moment. First, however, just think about what is required to move toward your short-term goals. Don't worry about whether this will be easy or difficult, just consider what would be required.

When planning your actions, it helps to be as specific as possible. For example, if your long-term goal is to have a wider circle of friends, a short-term goal might be to "get to know Karen better." A specific action to move you toward this short-term goal could be to "call Karen and invite her to go to a movie." To be even more specific, you might make a list of movies that you want to see.

The next step is to pick a time and place when you will carry out the action. By fixing the action in time and space, you move it from the realm of ideas (inside your head) into the realm of reality. For example, if you are going to call Karen to invite her to see a movie, you might do it tonight at 6:00 P.M., from home.

EXERCISE 8.6: Plan Actions

1. On the Value Map, where you wrote out your long-term and short-term goals related to a core value, list actions that you could take today or in the coming week to move you in the direction of one of your short-term goals.

2. Be very specific about the actions you will take.

3. Select a specific day and time when you can complete the first action on the list. Write the date and time, along with where you will complete the action, next to the action.

Actions & Goals

It is important to understand the relationship between your actions and your goals, especially if time is a factor. When the relationship between an action and a goal is complex, movement may not be readily apparent. Suppose you have a sinus infection. You visit your doctor, and she prescribes an antibiotic. Getting home with your prescription, you take a pill, then immediately take your temperature. If you find that you still have a fever, would you throw out the rest of the pills? "This antibiotic doesn't work! I've been misdiagnosed!" A clear understanding of how the action of taking the drug is related to the goal of reducing your fever can help you to maintain your commitment to sustained action. Perhaps a more common example is the relationship between dieting and losing weight. After two days of eating salads and skipping dessert, a dieter stepping onto the scale might find that her actions have not brought her closer to her goal (or have even moved the scale in the wrong direction!). A failure to understand the complex relationship between caloric intake and weight loss could result in a Big Mac Attack. Finally, consider the relationship between the actions of meeting new people and dating and the goal of finding a committed, long-term relationship. The person who says, "I've tried dating several people, but no relationships came of it" may be oversimplifying the relationship between dating and finding a relationship that works.

Being committed to sustained action is especially important when your goal is to acquire a new skill. The actions of buying groceries and following a recipe may not lead directly to the goal of cooking a delicious gourmet meal. Often the complexity of the relationship between actions and goals requires sustained action and perhaps setting additional short-term or sub-goals.

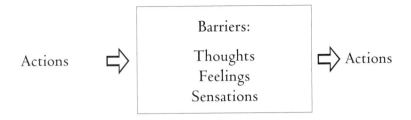

Figure 8.1: Actions and Barriers: Outside and Inside

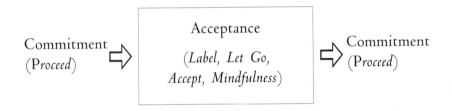

Figure 8.2: Acceptance and Commitment: Outside and Inside

Barriers to Action

So, you have set clear, obtainable long-term and short-term goals and have broken these down into specific actions that you can take. You have even planned the specific time and place that you will carry out those actions. So now it's just a matter of following through on your plans, right? Unfortunately, if it were as simple as that, you probably wouldn't be reading this book. For many people, especially those who have trouble with anxiety and worry, this is where things tend to get stuck. Even if you were successful in identifying valued directions, setting goals, and identifying and planning actions that move you in those valued directions, you still may come upon barriers to actually taking those actions. These can include both barriers on the outside and barriers on the inside.

Outside barriers include the practical problems that inevitably come up as we proceed toward a goal. It is impossible to predict all of the circumstances that might arise as we move our actions from the realm of ideas into the real world. These outside barriers are so common that they are really the constant in the equation of taking action. Commitment to the process of moving toward a goal almost always means problem solving and adjusting planned actions and short-term goals to accommodate and overcome unplanned obstacles. Chapter 10 looks at a number of skills (planning, problem solving, time management, assertiveness) that everyone can develop to help them in overcoming or working around these external barriers.

While outside barriers are a given, it is the inside or psychological barriers that are often the more crucial variable. The thoughts, feelings, and sensations that you experience as you contemplate and actually take action become barriers when you procrastinate, avoid, or stop action in order to escape from them. Accepting, defusing from, and proceeding *with* these barriers are what the first seven chapters of this book have been about.

Remember the outside/inside model? While actions are the things that you do on the outside, many of the perceived barriers to action occur on the inside (figure 8.1). While using the goal setting and planning skills presented in this chapter to commit and proceed in valued directions (the "P" in the LLAMP process), you will be using the first four steps of LLAMP to notice, accept, and defuse from your own personal inside barriers to committed action (figure 8.2).

Passengers on the Bus

Another way to think about these potential barriers is as passengers on the bus. Remember this metaphor from chapter 3? Having explored values in more detail, you may better understand the chosen route in the metaphor as your commitment to move in a valued direction. The actions you take as part of that commitment are the stops that the bus makes. The thoughts, feelings, and sensations that are potential barriers to action are all of the passengers that get onto the bus at those stops.

For many, these passengers are the same ones that were barriers to setting goals. Committing to one action can mean losing the option of taking others, which can be frightening. You might fear that you are choosing the wrong action or that you will fail. Other passengers include fears specific to the action being taken, fears of what others will think, or judgments about your abilities or readiness for action. For worriers, these barriers/passengers usually include fears related to the uncertainty of how things will turn out. In addition to a wide range of emotions and all of the physical sensations associated with anxiety, there are the thoughts about possible negative outcomes. "What if …" thoughts, ruminations on the past, and urges to engage in worry behavior can all act as barriers to proceeding with committed, value-directed action. Ultimately, our willingness to take action depends on our ability to turn these barriers into passengers. Willingness means proceeding on our valued route, making all of the stops that we have committed to, and having all of these passengers along for the ride.

EXERCISE 8.7: Identifying Barriers

1. On your Value Map, make a list of the inside barriers to action that you become aware of as you contemplate each action on your list.

2. Write down any thoughts that come up that might cause you to hesitate or avoid taking action. Include any "What if …" thoughts, doubts, or judgments.

3. Include any emotions that you are aware of as you look at your list of actions and imagine yourself carrying them out. In addition to anxiety, other feelings like sadness, anger, guilt, and boredom can all be barriers to taking action.

4. Notice any bodily sensations that you become aware of as you think about taking action. Add these to your list of barriers.

PROCEEDING IN THE RIGHT DIRECTION

In identifying the barriers to valued action, you likely listed many of the same thoughts, feelings, and bodily sensations that you identified in the labeling exercises in chapter 4. These are the passengers on the bus, the experiences on the inside of the box, or what is there to be accepted. As you proceed with valued actions, notice and label these experiences. Next, let go of the impulse to control them by taking a deep breath and reminding yourself to let go of the rope or lean into your thoughts and feelings. Accept whatever you are aware of on the inside by identifying with your observer self, experiencing thoughts and feelings in a defused way. At the same time, be mindful of all of your experience, grounding yourself in the present moment by paying attention to external as well as internal experience. Finally, continue to proceed with the action and series of actions that you are committed to.

This committed action is what distinguishes caring for all that is important in your life from simply worrying about it. In this chapter, you have started the process of considering exactly what you do care about or value and recognizing your response-ability or ability to respond by living a life consistent with those values. While values provide a direction to move toward, setting long-term and short-term goals can mobilize and focus your actions, keeping you on track. Committing to actions means fixing them in time and space through planning then proceeding to carry out those actions. During this process, try to remain mindful and accepting of all that is involved with your experience, allowing potential barriers to become passengers on the bus and taking them along for the ride. In the next chapter, you will practice applying all of the steps of the LLAMP approach to a wide range of internal experiences and begin to engage in some of the valued activities that you may have been avoiding until now.

CHAPTER NINE

TURNING ON THE LLAMP

Now that you have become more familiar with each step of the LLAMP process, it's time to put all of the steps together and to practice and develop your new skills. You may be surprised to hear that the best way (perhaps the only way) to learn a new approach to anxiety and worry is to practice feeling anxious and worried. Professionals who treat anxiety problems refer to this intentional, purposeful practice of experiencing certain thoughts and feelings as *exposure*.

WHY EXPOSURE?

Research has consistently shown that exposure of some sort is a crucial component of successful treatment for any type of anxiety problem (Foa and Kozak 1985). As you develop and implement your own program of exposure, it is important to keep in mind why you are doing so. The purpose of exposure is not to reduce your anxiety or to take anything else away from your experience. Rather, exposure is an opportunity to add the elements of acceptance and mindfulness to your experience. You can think of exposure as a "willingness workout" that will allow you to develop the willingness to think, feel, and experience (inside willingness) as well as the willingness to act (outside willingness).

Two Types of Exposure

Your exposure program will consist of two parts, each involving a different type of exposure. The first type, *worry exposure*, focuses on developing inside willingness. In other words the willingness to think worry thoughts, feel anxiety and other emotions related to worry, and to experience physical sensations, judgments, or urges to engage in worry-related behavior. When practicing worry exposure, your focus will be on using and developing the first four steps of the LLAMP approach: labeling, letting go, acceptance, and mindfulness. However, by committing to worry exposure and proceeding with it as something that moves you in a valued direction, you will be practicing the final step as well.

The second part of your exposure program will involve *taking action*. Here, the emphasis is on that final step of proceeding in the right direction. Taking action will involve all of the inside willingness of the worry exposure, with an added emphasis on outside willingness. This is the willingness to act. By committing to and engaging in valued activity, you will also develop a greater sense of response-ability in relation to your values.

What Makes It Exposure?

When you practice exposure, it's important to understand the purpose and nature of what you're doing. Otherwise, it is possible to go through the motions of an exposure program without experiencing actual exposure to worry and anxiety. As you proceed, keep the following points in mind.

Exposure without anxiety is not exposure.   Researchers have tried to determine what it is that makes exposure successful as a treatment for anxiety problems. In repeated studies, the actual activation of the fight-or-flight response has been found to be a crucial factor. Clinical studies have found that those individuals who benefit the most show increased heart rates when beginning exposure. Those who showed fewer signs of reactivity during exposure benefited less from treatment (Lang, Melamed, and Hart 1970; Borkovec and Sides 1979; Watson and Marks 1971). The reasons for this are not so mysterious when you consider the practical question of exactly what you are being exposed to. If the purpose is to practice or develop a new and different response to anxiety, it makes sense that you would have to be exposed to anxiety. If you reassure yourself or take other steps to reduce your anxiety during exposure, you may not actually be exposed. As you practice exposure, one of your goals will be to heighten and focus on your feelings of anxiety.

Exposure is always intentional. Often, when presented with the opportunity to practice experiencing anxiety and worry through exposure, worriers respond by saying something like this: "I don't need to intentionally seek out exposure. I get plenty of exposure already without even trying to. I experience anxiety and worry every day just going about my life. That's exposure enough." The problem with this statement is that it misses an essential aspect of what exposure is. By definition, exposure is intentional and purposeful. Exposure is something you *do*. On purpose. It's not something that just happens to you. Happening upon anxiety or worry is different from going out looking for it. The reason for this comes back to willingness. When you intentionally choose to engage in exposure, inherent in that intentionality is willingness. When we choose to do something, especially something optional, we are expressing willingness to act as well as to experience what goes along with that action. Exposure helps you to develop willingness, in part because it is intentional.

Exposure is always 100 percent. As you plan your exposure program, you will be setting your own parameters for each experience. You will choose which worry themes to work on when doing worry exposure. When it comes to taking action, you will decide how much or how long you will engage in a particular action. As you proceed, it may help to go slowly at first. The way to do this is to limit these parameters, not to limit the amount of anxiety that you are willing to feel. Exposure means being willing to experience 100 percent of the anxiety that is there to be experienced, no matter how high it goes. Remember the little experiment described in chapter 2 where you were hooked up to a machine that measured your anxiety on a scale of 0 to 100? The paradox of control illustrated by this story is that as long as you are trying to control or get rid of your anxiety, you are going to have it. You can't be a little bit willing to feel. Approaching exposure with the willingness to feel your anxiety "as long as it stays below 80" is not likely to change your experience of anxiety any more than if you set the limit at 40 or 10. For each exercise, set the situational and time parameters based on what you think you're ready for. Then complete the exercise with the willingness to feel 100 percent of your anxiety, even if it goes all the way up to 100 on the scale.

WORRY EXPOSURE

The first part of your exposure program is worry exposure. This is where you will set aside time every day to work on all of the skills presented in this book. As you practice worry exposure, you will not only be developing skills, you will be changing the context of your experience of worry and anxiety from one of control to one of willingness.

Make Time for Worry Exposure

To begin your exposure program, you will need to set aside a minimum of thirty minutes every day. If you have a busy schedule, this may present a challenge. In making the commitment to practice worry exposure every day, it will help to keep in mind the reasons why you picked up this book in the first place. Are you ready to do what it takes to change the way anxiety and worry work in your life? Would this move you in a valued direction? Start by committing to thirty minutes of daily practice for thirty days, then check in to see how you're doing. If you find that you are more willing to think, feel, and experience as well as more willing to act, you may decide to reduce the frequency of your worry exposure.

Rank Your Worry Themes

Begin by looking at the list of worry themes and sample worry thoughts that you identified in chapter 4 (exercise 4.5). You may want to add to this list to make it more complete. Look at the barriers to action that you identified on your Value Maps in the last chapter (exercise 8.7) and include any worry themes that act as barriers to valued action. Next to each theme, rank the amount of anxiety that you associate with that theme on a scale of 0 to 100, with 100 being the highest level of anxiety. If you find that all of your worry themes rank close to 100, you might want to break some of them down into less daunting subthemes. For example, say one of your themes is finances, and this includes worries about current living expenses, debt, and saving for retirement. You might separate this into two themes, one that triggers more anxiety (living expenses and debt) and one that triggers less anxiety (retirement planning). When you begin your daily practice of worry exposure, start with themes that are associated with lower levels of anxiety. As you get more practice applying the LLAMP approach, move on to the more challenging themes.

Play the Movie All the Way Through

Pick a theme and try to focus your thoughts on worries related to that theme. "What if ..." thoughts are often a good place to start. Allow yourself to imagine the worst-case scenario related to this theme, focusing on both thoughts and images. Let your thoughts get carried away toward the worst possible outcomes imaginable. For most worriers, once this process gets started, the familiar experience of worrying tends to kick in, and the thoughts come more naturally and automatically. For example, if one of your worry themes has to do with the possibility of losing your job, begin by focusing on specific situations that might lead to losing your job. What if you make a serious mistake and get fired? What if you get laid off? Then imagine how you might get the news. Would your boss tell you? What would this be like? Next, think about what it would be like to be unemployed. What if you were unable to find another job for a long time? What would happen to your financial situation? What other consequences might there be?

Stay with the Thoughts or Images

As you think through the worst-case scenario related to a worry theme, notice your anxiety level. Try to identify the thoughts or images that are associated with the highest level of anxiety. In the example above, it might be the image of your boss saying "You're fired!" or the thought of losing your home because you are unable to pay the rent or mortgage. When you find that image or thought that triggers the strongest feelings of anxiety, stay with that image or thought, focusing on it and allowing your anxiety to increase as much as possible.

Stay with the thoughts and feelings until the end of your thirty minutes of worry exposure. If you find that the theme that you are working on does not trigger much anxiety or that the anxiety subsides after a while, pick another worry theme from your list and work with that one.

Make a Worry Tape

If you have trouble activating anxiety when you begin doing worry exposure, or if you have trouble generating worry thoughts and applying the LLAMP approach at the same time, it may help to make a worry tape. Using a tape recorder, make a tape of yourself worrying out loud about one of your worry themes. Simply say your worry thoughts out loud and describe the images and scenarios that are part of your worry. As you do so, express the sense of anxiety and urgency behind these thoughts with your voice. Make a separate tape for each of your worry themes. Each tape should be about fifteen minutes long. During your worry exposure sessions, you can listen to the same tape twice or listen to two different tapes. Focus on the thoughts expressed in the tape, being mindful of thoughts, feelings, and sensations that you experience while listening to it. You may find that it's easier to hold the observer perspective and defuse from the thoughts on the tape recorder than it is to defuse from thoughts that are solely in your head. If this is the case, consider listening to worry tapes as a place to start, and work up to doing worry exposure without the tapes.

Use Your Skills

During the exposure session, as soon as you are aware of anxiety and feel yourself getting into the process of worrying, begin to implement the LLAMP approach.

Label your thoughts and feelings as "worry." The purpose of this step is to help you to notice and identify when you are worrying in daily life. When doing the exposure exercises, it is sort of an academic step, since worrying is what you are setting out to do. It is still helpful to practice labeling the experience as "worry" if only to build an association between the actual process of worry and the label.

Let go of control. Even though you will be intentionally generating worry thoughts, you may still have trouble giving these thoughts free reign. You are even more likely to notice an impulse to control feelings of anxiety or physical sensations as they arise. Use your letting-go skills to let go of this struggle and lean into your anxiety. Remember that this step is not about getting relaxed or letting go of anxiety or any other feeling. It is about letting go of the struggle with those feelings. Metaphorically, it is about letting go of the shovel (the man-in-the-hole metaphor) or letting go of the rope (the monster-and-the-rope metaphor). Taking a deep breath, relaxing your muscles, and thinking "let go" can all help you to keep your hands off of your anxiety. Let go and feel what you are feeling.

Accept and observe worry thoughts. That is, experience them in a defused way. As your worry thoughts begin to come more automatically, notice the separation between you and your thoughts, recognizing your thoughts as content and your self as context. Notice that the Observer You is bigger than your worries, which are only part of your experience. Panning back, notice that you are the art, not the ant (art vs. ant metaphor). Observe your thoughts as thoughts. Don't argue with them or get involved with them. Let them move past like a river or a conveyor belt. You may want to use one or more of the defusion exercises from chapter 6 to help you experience these thoughts as thoughts, separate from their referents.

Mindfulness of the present moment. Maintaining the perspective of the Observer You, as you focus on your worry thoughts, notice and make room for other thoughts, feelings, and bodily sensations. Deliberately become aware of all aspects of your experience in the current moment. Notice any judgments about how you are doing, or urges to stop doing the exercise. In particular, be aware of all the ways that your mind may try to reassure you or otherwise help you avoid feeling what is there to be felt. As you continue to observe your thoughts and feelings, allow yourself to also be aware of where you are. Notice sounds, sights, scents, and other sensations. If you like, do a quick body scan or spend a moment observing your breathing. Remember that this is not about distracting yourself from the worry and anxiety. Hold the worry thoughts and anxious feelings in your awareness and make room for the rest of your experience as well.

Proceed in the right direction. As you practice acceptance and mindfulness of all that is involved in your experience of worry exposure, maintain your commitment to practicing for the full thirty minutes. If you give in to the urge to interrupt the exposure or find yourself engaging in subtle avoidance like reassuring or distracting yourself, remember that you are committing to a process, not an outcome, and just resume the exposure. When the time comes each day to practice exposure, be mindful of any inside barriers that may arise, and remember that commitment means taking action. Part of what you're developing by doing worry exposure is the willingness to act, turning these potential barriers into passengers and taking them along for the ride.

With time, you will begin to apply the steps of the LLAMP process in a more fluid way. You may notice that you go back and forth between the steps or find that they begin to overlap and merge. This is natural and is a sign that you are making the skills your own. The LLAMP sequence is presented in steps to provide a structure for learning the skills and principles involved. As they become part of your natural response to anxiety and worry, the structure will become secondary to the actual experience of willingness.

TAKING ACTION

The second part of your exposure program will consist of beginning to carry out the valued actions that you identified in chapter 8. These are actions that move you toward the short-term and long-term goals that align with your core values. Proceeding with valued action will provide exposure to the very barriers that you identified in exercise 8.7, as well as to some that you did not anticipate. Exposure to these barriers will allow you to further develop not only your willingness to think, feel, and experience but your willingness to act as well. Taking action while practicing the LLAMP approach, you will transform these barriers into passengers on the bus, proceeding with them in valued directions.

Look at Your Value Maps

Take a careful look at the Value Maps that you created for each of your core values in chapter 8. Look at the actions that you listed when completing exercise 8.6. Notice the times and places that you planned for each of these actions when doing that exercise. Have any of the times that you set aside for action already gone by? Were you able to proceed with action as planned? If not, what barriers did you encounter? If necessary, make adjustments to the times that you previously set for these actions. Make sure there are at least some actions that you can take immediately. Make a schedule of the actions you are going to take over the next two weeks. You may want to use a calendar to do this. If there is too much going on, break the actions down into smaller subactions, scheduling some now and saving some for later. Be aware that you are making a commitment as you do this. It's fine to go slow at first, scheduling only those actions that you are ready to commit to.

Start Now

The best time to begin taking action is now. Don't feel that you have to master the LLAMP approach through worry exposure before beginning to take action. You can start both parts of your exposure program at the same time. In fact, these two types of exposure can complement one another. For example, as you are taking action during the day, you may encounter a specific worry that appears to be a barrier. You can make a note of this worry and work with it during your worry exposure session that night. Similarly, worry exposure can serve as a rehearsal for applying the LLAMP approach when you are taking action.

Use Your Skills

As you proceed and follow through with the activities that you have committed to, be on the lookout for worry thoughts and other potential barriers. When they show up, proceed with the action you have committed to while applying the LLAMP steps. Label the thoughts and feelings as worry, let go of the urge to control or get rid of these thoughts and feelings, accept your thoughts by observing them in a defused way, be mindful of the present moment and all that it includes, and proceed with the valued activity.

If You Fail

Remember that you are committing to a process, not an outcome. If and when you fail to follow through on a planned action, it is your commitment to this process that will allow you to reschedule the activity and carry on. Even if you follow through on all of your plans, your actions will sometimes produce results other than those that you intended. You may find yourself moving in the wrong direction at times. Remember that paths that take you in a valued direction are not always straight. If you become discouraged or confused about your goals, revisit your list of core values. Make sure that the goals you have chosen are still serving these values. Adjust your plans for action to accommodate any new information and renew your commitment. Using your skills, proceed in the right direction.

MOVING FORWARD

As you proceed with valued activities, practicing your skills and developing inside and outside willingness along the way, continue to plan and schedule those action steps that move you toward your goals. As you do this, you are likely to encounter some barriers to moving forward that are more external than internal. The final chapter of this book will look at how you can develop and build several skill areas that will help you to address these external barriers.

CHAPTER TEN

SKILL BUILDING & TROUBLESHOOTING

After reading and working on the exercises in this book, you have likely gained a greater understanding of the interaction between worry thoughts, anxiety, and worry behaviors. Practicing the LLAMP approach, you may already have found yourself more willing to experience thoughts and feelings that have been barriers to taking action in important areas of your life. With the help of the values clarification exercises in chapter 8, you may have a clearer idea of exactly what those actions include.

If you are like many worriers, however, you may still have trouble with certain practical aspects of planning and taking action. People who engage in excessive worry often have a long history of feeling overwhelmed by problems that arise and are unable to come up with possible solutions. In chapter 4, we looked at how worriers can confuse worrying with problem solving and planning. Even when they are able to come up with a possible solution and a plan to implement it, some people have trouble sticking with that plan because they are not skilled at managing their time. Finally, problems with being assertive can lead some individuals to overcommit and to avoid asking for the help they need to get things done. The difficulties that worriers have with these skills can leave them feeling confused and overwhelmed by the many demands in their lives. Unable to respond effectively to these demands, these individuals instead respond with worry. This final chapter presents some basic strategies for improving your skills in each of the following areas: planning, time management, problem solving, and assertiveness.

PLANNING

You may find that when you are spending a great deal of time worrying about a certain aspect of your life or an upcoming event, it helps to do some planning in this area. Spending time going over possible outcomes over and over again in your mind or considering the various things that might go wrong is not planning. Remember, the litmus test for determining whether you are engaged in a process of planning or worrying is the outcome of that process. If the outcome is a list of actions or reasonable precautions that you can take, then you are planning. If the outcome is an increase in anxiety and behaviors like checking, procrastination, and avoidance, you are worrying. What the two processes have in common is that they begin with thinking about and imagining future events. When this process heads down the road toward worry, it's usually because the focus is more on factors that are beyond your control (what might happen) than on the actions that you can take.

Make a Reasonable Actions List

Imagining the future can be a helpful way to prepare for taking action. One way to make sure that you are planning and not worrying is to make a list of the actions you can take. By imagining and listing the actions you intend to take, you can determine the best way to sequence activities and anticipate any problems that may arise. When you become aware of a potential problem, you may be able to think of precautions that you can take to minimize the possibility of a negative outcome. If so, add these precautions to your list of reasonable actions. Having a reasonable actions list is a helpful way to determine the limits of planning and the beginning of worry. As long as you are keeping up with your reasonable actions list, you are doing all that you can reasonably do. If you find that you have taken all of the actions on your list but are still thinking about a situation or event, you have moved beyond planning and have begun worrying. For example, say you are planning to move. Your reasonable actions list might include packing, hiring movers, arranging to pick up keys for your new home, etc. Once you have made the list, if you notice that you are having thoughts about your upcoming move, ask yourself the following question: "Is this something that I can add to my reasonable actions list?" If the answer is yes, add the item to your list. If the answer is no, then the thought is a worry thought. So, if you are having a thought like "Will I have power and phone service on the day I move in?" it suggests an item for your reasonable actions list: "Call power and phone companies to order services." Suppose this item is already on your list, and you are having thoughts like "What if there are problems with getting power and phone service started?" Is this something you can add to your reasonable actions list? Is there anything more than calling to order services that you can reasonably do? Probably not. So, thinking about this item any longer is not planning, it's worrying.

Plan in Small Steps

When faced with large or complex tasks, it is easy to feel overwhelmed and discouraged. Planning allows us to break large tasks down into smaller, more manageable steps. Consider the task of finding a new job. As anyone who has faced this challenge knows, the thought of finding a new job can be daunting. The very idea is an invitation to a festival of worries, such as "What if there are no jobs available?" "What if I'm not qualified?" and "What about references?" Focusing on the larger goal of finding a new job can trigger worry thoughts, heightened anxiety, and escape behavior like procrastination. Planning means asking yourself the question "What are the steps involved in finding a new job?" By answering this question, you will be able to list smaller, more manageable actions that you can take. For example:

1. Revise resumé

2. Look at job listings

3. Draft cover letter

4. Contact references

If you sit down at the computer and say to yourself, "I need to find a new job," you may find yourself at a loss for where to begin. Your response may be paralysis, heading for the refrigerator, or heading out the door. On the other hand, if you say to yourself, "Right now I will revise my resumé," you at least have a sense of how to begin and how long this job will take you.

Any task can be broken down into a series of smaller steps. If you find that you are overwhelmed by the thought of cleaning the house, you can plan to clean up specific rooms. If it's time to do your taxes, perhaps you can start by just getting your documentation and receipts together, then complete your paperwork in small sections. The laundry gets done one load at a time, a wall gets painted one coat at a time, and books are written one chapter at a time. When you start to break things down into smaller tasks, you may notice thoughts like "I should be able to do more than that" or "I would rather get it all over with at once." The question is, are these thoughts helping you to take action? Or are they barriers to getting started?

Marry Each Step with a Specific Time

In chapter 8 you learned the importance of fixing actions in time and space as a way to move them from the realm of ideas into the realm of reality. After you have broken a task down into steps, it's important to plan a specific time for completing each step.

Use a calendar.   This is perhaps the most helpful bit of technology for people who have a lot to get done, provided you use it correctly. If you have not used a calendar before, it's probably a good idea to start simply. Large, bulky day planners with complex organizational tools and lots of high-tech toys can obscure the essential function of a calendar as a way of marrying time and activity. Your calendar should be small enough to carry around but large enough to write things in. The kind that allows you to look at one week at a time makes sense for most people. Also, you only need one calendar. You might be surprised at the number of people who go from using no calendar at all to using two or more. In their exuberance they think, "If one calendar is good, two calendars will be even better!" Others use both a paper calendar and a calendar on their personal computer. Having to remember which calendar to look in for which information to avoid double-booking defeats the essential functions of a calendar as a way to centralize information and allocate time for action.

Schedule time to take specific actions.   When you schedule what you are going to do when, be realistic. One of the most common mistakes that people make when planning is to schedule too much in too short of a time frame. Allow time for breaks, and don't worry about finishing a task early and having time left over. It's better to have extra time to get a head start on things that are scheduled for later than to feel that you are constantly running behind the overly ambitious schedule that you have set for yourself. Setting reasonable and obtainable goals encourages a feeling of success and achievement, which is necessary for the long haul. Planning to do too much sets you up for feeling like a failure, which can make a potentially rewarding task a negative experience.

Don't be afraid to reschedule.   When making plans, always use a pencil! Life is complicated and does not always proceed as planned. When external, practical events prevent you from following your original plan, don't give up on the planning process altogether. Instead of just blowing off a plan that isn't working out, revise the plan. If something comes up or you're not able to finish some task in the allotted time, reschedule the task for another time, writing it in your calendar.

Be careful of overplanning.   While spending some time planning can help you to get things done more efficiently, too much time spent planning can actually interfere with the process of getting things done. A common mistake is the overly detailed to-do list. Even someone with minimal responsibilities who lists everything that they need to get done is likely to feel overwhelmed before even beginning. If possible, avoid to-do lists altogether, scheduling things directly into your calendar. If it is January and you think of something that needs to be done sometime in April, it's fine to make a note of it in the margin of your calendar at the beginning of April. When April arrives, you can plan and schedule the details. If you do feel the need for a to-do list, try to limit it to things that you are likely to forget, and by all means limit yourself to one list. Occasionally, when you have several small tasks that need to be done in a short period of time, it may help to make a to-do list of today's tasks that can be discarded on the same day it is created.

TIME MANAGEMENT

While planning skills involve taking in the big picture of goals and breaking these down into actions, time management has to do with how you proceed with actions on the ground, moving from the plan to getting started and continuing through to the completion of tasks. The best planning in the world will not be helpful if you are unable to manage your time well on an hour-by-hour basis. People who worry a lot can feel overwhelmed by the demands of day-to-day tasks, obligations, and deadlines. Worry can magnify the impact of these ordinary stressors and interfere with the ability to get things done.

Look at Your Calendar Daily

This point can't be stressed enough. One of the reasons for having a calendar is so that you do not have to rely on your memory. So don't rely on your memory. Look at your calendar at least once a day. A good practice is to look at your calendar at the beginning and end of every day. By having a few minutes of calendar time at the end of the day, you will be reminded of what you are doing tomorrow before going to bed tonight. This will allow for any necessary preparations (like setting an alarm clock) and prevent any last-minute surprises. A quick look in the morning will refresh your memory and help to get you on track for the day.

Use Mindfulness to Stay On Task

Often when there is a lot to be done, it is easy to become distracted from the task at hand by thinking about and worrying about what needs to be done next, or even tasks that lie further into the future. Worrying about future tasks while doing the current task is like doing two tasks at once, one with your hands and one with your head. Not only is this a drain on your energy, but it can also lead to slower and poorer performance of everything that you do. Once you have planned the sequence of tasks that you wish to complete, allow yourself to do each task mindfully. Focus your attention on what you are doing, allowing yourself to be aware of all aspects of the present experience. Notice the pull toward the past or the future in your thoughts, and try to stay with the present moment. If you're concerned about not having time to complete everything you have planned and need to reschedule some tasks or to problem solve, try to do this in between tasks rather than during. Far from taking more time, planning while you are planning and working while you are working is likely to lead to more efficient use of your time and energy.

Break the Day into Sections

As you tackle your plans for the day, it can help to approach the day in two or three parts. Before lunch and after lunch is a good approach, or morning, afternoon, and evening. This way, each part of the day has its own objectives. If you are at work, know what you want to accomplish before lunch and what you will tackle after lunch. Remember to be realistic in setting your goals.

Take breaks and mini breaks. It is important to reward yourself for concerted effort by taking breaks. Larger breaks like going to lunch or taking a long walk can break the day into sections, allowing you time to experience a sense of achievement for the parts of a task you have completed. In addition to longer breaks, short mini breaks can also help you to be more productive. Interrupting work to stretch, take a short walk, or to make a brief phone call can allow you to return to a task with a sense of renewed energy.

Return from your breaks. Crucial to taking effective breaks is making sure that they are not too frequent and don't last too long. Try to set small goals to complete before your next break. Then, before walking away from your task, specify when you will return to it.

Build a Bridge from One Activity to the Next

One way to keep breaks from stopping the flow of activity is to build a bridge to the next activity before taking a break. Instead of interrupting your work immediately after finishing one part of a task, take a few preliminary steps toward beginning the next part before taking a break. This way, when you return from the break, you will know exactly where to begin and can jump right in. For example, if you are writing a report and finish one section, you might write the first sentence or two of the next section before taking a break. If you have just finished folding your underwear and your next task is to iron your shirts, you might set up the ironing board and lay out the shirts that you plan to iron before taking a break. Getting started on a task is often the hardest part. Bridging tasks saves you the time you might otherwise spend deciding what to do next or where to begin. You can also do this with larger, more complex tasks by bridging today's work with tomorrow's or this week's with next week's.

Sequence for Success (The "Premack Principle")

Another way to increase your productivity is to use activities that you tend to do often as a reward for doing those activities that never seem to get done. This strategy of rewarding low-frequency behavior with the opportunity to engage in high-frequency behavior is also known as the *Premack Principle*, after the behavioral researcher who first wrote about it (1962). It has also been called "Grandma's Rule." Basically, it says "*first* take out the garbage, *then* you can play video games" or "*first* eat your vegetables, *then* you can have dessert." Suppose you have a highly valued but low-frequency behavior like exercising and a high-frequency behavior like watching television. The Premack Principle would suggest that you plan to watch television after exercising instead of the other way around.

While this sounds like common sense (and it is), people often fail to pay attention to how they sequence tasks. For example, suppose you have four things you would like to do when you get home this evening: pay some bills, call a friend, clean the bathroom, and watch some TV. If you are like most people, the way you sequence these four activities will be a crucial factor in whether or not they all get done. What is likely to happen if you take them on in the following sequence?

1. Call friend

2. Watch some TV

3. Clean bathroom

4. Pay bills

The pleasurable activity of watching TV could likely fill up the evening, helping you to avoid the last two activities. A better approach might be to reverse the sequence. The only problem with this, however, is that the rewards may be too long in coming. The prospect of paying the bills *and* cleaning the bathroom may be so daunting that you put off starting either. Also, after paying the bills, you are likely to want a break before tackling the bathroom. If we use the Premack Principle and alternate low-frequency tasks with high-frequency rewards, we get a sequence that looks like this:

1. Pay bills

2. Call friend

3. Clean bathroom

4. Watch some TV

In this sequence, you get the very low frequency behavior of paying those bills out of the way and then immediately reward yourself by calling your friend. This is a time-limited activity, however, and is followed by cleaning the bathroom *before* starting the potentially unlimited activity of watching TV.

PRIORITIZE ACTIVITIES

All activities are not of equal value, and some are more urgent than others. When you consider what you have planned to accomplish each day, recognize that each activity can be ranked on two dimensions: value and urgency.

Do urgent tasks first. When prioritizing activities or tasks, it's okay to begin by focusing more on urgency. One way to do this is to rank each item as follows:

Priority A: Extremely urgent, must be done today

Priority B: Must be done soon, but not necessarily today

Priority C: Must be done eventually

If you are running short on time, try to complete all of the Priority A items first. Notice that today's Priority B items will become

Priority A tomorrow. Priority C items can be rescheduled for a less hectic day.

Be careful about those Priority C items.   Often the tasks or activities that are least urgent are also the ones that are of the most value in our lives. Activities like spending time with loved ones, experiencing nature, relaxing, and learning something new are rarely seen as urgent but can be very valuable. Pay attention to any activities that keep getting postponed, and work on a plan to make time for them. One way to address this is to build a day or an afternoon into your regular schedule that is devoted specifically to these nonurgent but highly valuable activities.

WHAT DO YOU DO WHEN NOTHING GETS DONE?

When things don't get done as planned, pay attention to what happens instead. If you find that you got nothing done all morning, notice that you probably did do *something*. What was it? Noticing what you do when you fail to stick to your plan affords you the opportunity to problem solve and possibly avoid the same pitfalls in the future. If necessary, keep a log for a day or two of all of your activities. Analyze the log to see where you get blown off course. If you notice that checking your e-mail on a mini break leads to time-consuming exchanges that take you away from your plan, you might decide to check e-mail less frequently and later in the day, after completing tasks that you are likely to avoid. If you find yourself choosing to do things that seem more pressing than the planned task, perhaps you can plan a time to take on these pressing items that does not interfere with the task you are avoiding.

LIMIT "UNLIMITED" ACTIVITIES

We are surrounded by opportunities to engage in passive activities that can easily fill up unlimited amounts of time, precluding more active, productive, or fulfilling options. The average American household has multiple television sets, often with fifty-plus channels. Digital music players allow us to carry thousands of songs wherever we go. Personal computers offer us an ever-growing variety of games, information, and entertainment experiences. While media options can provide us with necessary stimulation, education, and even distraction, the problem lies in the unlimited nature of those options that exist today. It's possible to spend every one of your waking hours pointing, clicking, and channel surfing without exhausting the potentially interesting and engaging experiences available to consume your time. It is important to consider the value of these activities relative to other values in your life when deciding how much time to devote to them. Even more crucial is to make sure that you are in fact making a conscious decision about how much time you give to media options. If you are not clear about exactly how much time TV, music, games, and Web surfing fill in your daily life, it might be interesting to keep a log of how much time you spend engaged with these media for a week. How does this measure up to time spent on other activities that you value?

PROBLEM SOLVING

Researchers have found that people who have trouble with problem solving run into difficulty in two areas. First, they tend to view a problem in vague and overly general ways. Second, they tend to focus solely on the implications of the problem, failing to generate any possible solutions. This is what happened to Marty the pizza guy.

Marty the Pizza Guy

Marty had a job working as a pizza delivery driver. While he had to use his own car to make deliveries, his employer paid for gas. Between Marty's hourly wage and tips, he made more than enough money to meet his moderate living expenses. Things were going well for Marty, who had almost saved up enough money to buy the shiny new motorcycle he wanted, when the old car that he had been driving began to give him trouble. Twice in one month the car failed to start, causing Marty to miss work and to pay for towing and costly repairs. After the second time, his mechanic suggested that it might be time to get a new car. Marty had failed to see this coming. If he bought a new car, he would never be able to afford the motorcycle he had been saving for. Yet he

*absolutely had to have a car to deliver pizzas. A new car meant
no motorcycle, but no car meant no job, no income, and therefore
no motorcycle, no rent, no food, no life! As he made his deliveries,
Marty worried about how much longer his car would last.*
*He worried about what would happen if he had to miss any more
work. He had already dipped into his motorcycle savings to pay
for the last round of car repairs. If he had to miss work for
several days, he would need to use savings to make up the
difference when the rent came due. What if he used up his savings
on more car repairs and ended up having to junk the car anyway?
Then he would have no car and no money. He could end up out
on the street! When Marty thought about all of these problems his
chest felt tight, and he tightened his grip on the steering wheel.*
*His reflection in the rearview mirror revealed a brow marked with
beads of sweat and eyes that were dark pools of panic. "My whole
life is unraveling!" he thought. "This is the beginning of the end."*

Define the Problem

When thoughts about a problem are accompanied by anxiety, our
perception of the problem can become distorted. You may recall from
chapter 4 that this biased way of processing information, in which
threats can appear more global than they actually are, is called hypervigilance. If you perceive a problem in a vague and all-encompassing
way, you may feel so hopeless that you fail to even look for a solution.
This was the case for Marty.

Describe the problem as specifically as possible.   By defining the
parameters of the problem, you are establishing that it does have limits.
This can help you to feel more hopeful and to recognize what does and
does not need to be addressed. For example, if Marty were to clearly
define his problem, it would look something like this: "I can't rely on
my car any longer. I need a reliable car if I am going to continue to
deliver pizzas." Notice how this definition of the problem is limited to
the car and the requirements of his current job. This is much different
from Marty's vague and global thoughts about "all these problems."
When the problem is defined in these terms, it becomes clear that
what needs to be addressed is limited to the car or the job. Concerns
about income in general, paying rent, using up savings, and ending up

on the street do not need to be addressed and lie beyond the limits of the problem.

Break the problem into smaller segments. By separating the problem into its component parts, each component can be taken on in turn. Each part of a complex problem is likely to be more manageable than all of the parts combined. For example, Marty's problem involves the following components: car, job, and motorcycle. Taking on the car component first, he might consider whether he would need a car for anything other than his job. If he did not have to deliver pizzas, could he use public transportation until he was able to buy a motorcycle? Then, addressing the job component, Marty can consider how much he wants to keep the pizza job and what other options might be available. If he found a job that did not involve delivery and could buy a motorcycle, he may not need a car. Finally, there is the motorcycle component. Is the motorcycle important enough to consider a job change? If he had a nice new car, would he be willing to put off buying the motorcycle? When each aspect of the problem is addressed separately, the questions raised are simpler and easier to answer.

Brainstorm

Once you have a handle on the specific parameters of the problem, try to generate as many solutions as possible. This is called *brainstorming*. During this phase of problem solving, the goal is to come up with as many ideas as you can, not to evaluate the ideas. Don't worry about how odd or unreasonable any of the solutions may seem. Many people find that when they evaluate a solution and find it unworkable, they become discouraged and have trouble coming up with any other ideas. Brainstorming allows you to get as creative as possible without hampering the flow of ideas by making critical evaluations. For example, as Marty finally settled down and began to brainstorm, he came up with the following possible solutions:

= Buy a new car, pass on new motorcycle

= Buy a cheap used car, keep saving for new motorcycle

= Buy a cheap used car and a cheap used motorcycle

= Buy motorcycle and try to deliver pizzas on that

= Buy motorcycle, let roommate use in exchange for using his car for work

= Get a job where a car is not needed

= Double savings in Vegas, buy new car *and* new motorcycle

Compare Only Two Solutions at a Time

When you're done brainstorming, it's time to evaluate each of the possible solutions and to choose the best one. It is best to approach this in a systematic way by comparing only two solutions at a time. This way, you will not be overwhelmed by your own list of options. Compare two options, considering all of the pros and cons of pursuing each. Then, pick the best of the two options, discarding the less workable of the two. Next, pair the winning option with another option from your list of possible solutions, and repeat the process until you arrive at the best solution. When Marty started to compare the options listed above, he considered only two at a time, starting with two that were fairly similar:

= Buy a cheap used car, keep saving for new motorcycle

= Buy a cheap used car and a cheap used motorcycle

As he focused on just these two options, Marty realized that having the shiny new motorcycle that he had been dreaming of was very important to him and worth waiting for. If he did spend some of his savings on a cheap used car in order to keep his current job, he would keep saving until he could buy the new motorcycle that he really wanted. Marty eliminated the second option and kept the first one. Clarifying the importance of buying a *new* motorcycle made it easier for Marty to make the next comparison:

= Buy a cheap used car, keep saving for new motorcycle

= Buy motorcycle, let roommate use in exchange for using his car for work

Marty's roommate was a nice guy, but he was not the most responsible person in the world. If Marty was going to invest in the nice new motorcycle that he really wanted, he realized that he would not want his roommate driving it around while he was at work. He would rather wait for the new motorcycle than buy it now and have to share it. Again, he eliminated the second option of the pair. Marty continued with this process of comparing two options at a time until he was down to one solution that seemed to be the best of the bunch.

Remember Your Response-Ability

Sometimes when problems pop up unexpectedly, you may feel so surprised and taken aback that you have trouble shifting into problem-solving mode. You may have angry feelings about the problem based on the belief that the problem should not exist. This sort of thinking is not likely to be helpful. While you may wish that the problem didn't exist, there is no fundamental rule of the universe being broken when a problem arises. In fact, if there is a rule, it may be that problems will always arise eventually.

If you find yourself complaining about a problem extensively, to the exclusion of working toward finding a solution, it may reflect a belief that you are powerless to make changes or otherwise have an impact on events. While a certain amount of venting can release stress and help to elicit needed empathy and support from others, it is not likely to change the problem. It can help to remember that as an intelligent adult with verbal and reasoning abilities, you have the ability to respond to a problem in a number of different ways. Recognizing this fundamental response-ability can help you to transition from indignation and complaining to problem solving.

ASSERTIVENESS

A final factor that can contribute to worrying is a lack of assertive behavior. Individuals who don't know how to say no to requests or how to ask for what they need often end up with more on their plate than they can reasonably handle. A common response to this overload is anxiety and worry. If this sounds like you, learning to be more assertive could leave you with less to be worried about.

What Is Assertiveness?

Being assertive means clearly expressing your own feelings and needs while being respectful of the feelings and needs of others. When we are assertive, we are honest, direct, and firm without attacking or putting others down. We stand up for our own rights without trampling on the rights of others.

Being assertive is different from being aggressive. Many people avoid being assertive for fear of appearing aggressive. Aggressive behavior is characterized by an "I win, you lose" approach. It proceeds from the assumption that there is no way to stand up for my rights without violating yours. Therefore, when we are aggressive, we attack, imposing our wishes on others in a way that violates their rights.

Being assertive is the middle path. If you consider a continuum of ways to express your feelings and needs, with nonassertive behavior on the left and aggressive behavior on the right, assertive behavior would fall in the middle (figure 10.1). When you are nonassertive, you are self-denying, inhibited, and allow others to choose for you. When you are aggressive, you are self-enhancing at the expense of others, attacking, and tend to choose for others. Taking the middle path of assertiveness means being self-affirming, expressive, and choosing for yourself.

Assertiveness can be broken down into two essential skills: saying no to requests and asking for what you need. Delegating tasks is a related skill that involves being assertive.

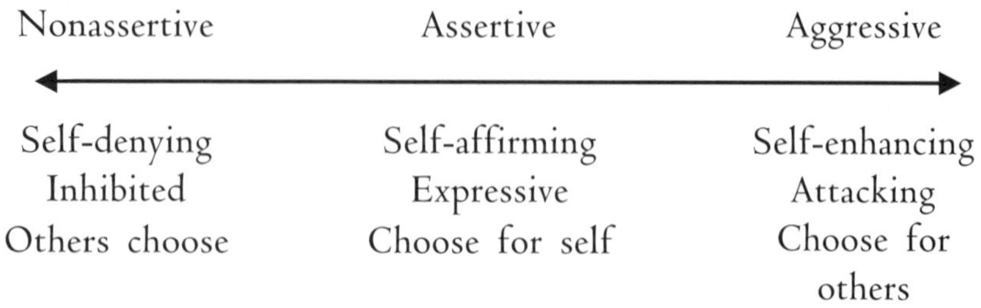

Nonassertive	Assertive	Aggressive
←		→
Self-denying	Self-affirming	Self-enhancing
Inhibited	Expressive	Attacking
Others choose	Choose for self	Choose for others

Figure 10.1: Assertiveness Is the Middle Path

Saying No

People who fail to say no to unexpected or unreasonable requests often have a number of beliefs or imaginary rules that make saying no difficult. Others may want to say no but not know exactly how to go about it. In either case, the failure to say no can lead to over-commitment and attempts to please others that interfere with following through on your own valued activities.

Barriers to saying no include beliefs about yourself and others. You may pride yourself on being "helpful" or believe that saying no means that you're being selfish or uncaring. When faced with a request, it helps to keep your core values in mind. Although being helpful may be one of your core values, there may be times when agreeing to a specific request is not compatible with other core values. For example, saying yes to a request to work late may be incompatible with the value of spending time with loved ones at home. There may be times when saying no can be just as helpful or more helpful than saying yes.

You may assume that others will be hurt, offended, or angered if you say no. At times, this may be the case. This is especially true if the person you are saying no to is used to hearing you say yes. Even when this is true, the hard feelings are usually short-lived and seldom persist once people adjust to your new assertiveness skills. More often, how-ever, the reactions others have to your no are not as severe as you may imagine. Think of the last time someone responded with a polite but clear no to a request that you made. How hurt, offended, or angry were you? How long did that feeling last?

There are many different ways to say no. Here are some possible variations that might be appropriate for different situations. Experiment, add your own touch, and find the no that works best for you:

= *The No-Frills No:*

"No, I won't be able to help you with that."

= *The Empathic No:*

"No. I know you were hoping I could help, but I just can't do it."

= *The Reason-Giving No:*

"No. I'll be working on a project at home this weekend."

= *The If-Only No:*

"No. If only I had known about it a little earlier, I could have said yes."

= *The Helpful No:*

"No. I can't help you, but have you considered trying _____ ?"

= *The Yes, but No No:*

"I can do *this*, no problem, but ... No, I won't be able to do *that*."

= *The Good Intentions No:*

"I'd really like to help you with that, but no, I can't."

= *The No-without-No No (for people in power, like your boss):*

"I'm very busy, so which of these responsibilities should take priority?"

The key to making any of these nos work is to mean it when you say it and to stand by it. If you use one of these no responses, and the person that you are speaking to ignores or challenges it, try saying it again in exactly the same way.

Practice saying no mindfully. If you have a long history of not saying no, it's probably a good idea to practice. Once you have decided that saying no makes sense in a given situation (in that it moves you in a valued direction and is therefore the thing to do), you might want to practice saying no by yourself or with someone that you trust. Test out some of the different nos listed above. When the time comes to actually say no to the person making a request or demand, doing so is likely to trigger all of the thoughts and feelings that have been barriers to saying no in the past. Apply the LLAMP approach to these thoughts and feelings, acknowledging them and observing them in a defused and mindful way even as you proceed with your commitment to saying no. It may help to start by practicing saying no to simple requests made by someone you trust. You can even let them know that you're practicing saying no. Notice any feelings of guilt or anxiety, as well as any self-judgments or thoughts about what the other person might be thinking. Let go of any effort to control or dispel these feelings and thoughts, allowing yourself to experience them as just thoughts, part of what happens when you say no. Be mindful of other aspects of your experience in the current moment, and proceed with your commitment to saying no.

Asking for What You Need

Another way to act assertively is by asking others for what you need. Sometimes this is a matter of making a simple request. At other times, it can involve setting limits on the behavior of others. You are setting limits when you say no to a request or demand. However, you can also set limits by making your own request, giving others feedback on how their behavior is affecting you, and stating what you would like for them to do differently.

There are three steps to asking for what you need:

1. Summarize the facts.

2. Indicate how you feel.

3. Ask for what you need.

A good time to ask for what you need is any time that others behave in ways that interfere with your personal rights or efforts to act in valued ways. For example, if you value having a tidy living area and are living with someone who leaves dirty articles of clothing lying all over the house, it may help to assertively ask for what you need.

Summarize the facts.   Start by objectively describing the situation that is problematic for you. Focus on the facts of the situation rather than expressing your opinions or judgments. This part of the message should be as nonemotional as possible. Don't exaggerate or over-generalize. Avoid excessively colorful descriptions or labels. Focus on describing *your* experience, using the word "I," rather than describing the behavior of the person you are talking to or using the word "you." For example, consider the differences in these two statements summarizing the dirty laundry problem described above:

Assertive:

"I sometimes find dirty socks on the coffee table and soiled shirts lying on the floor."

Aggressive:

"*You* always (overgeneralizing) leave your dirty, filthy, stinking (excessive description) clothes lying everywhere (exaggeration), you disgusting slob (labeling)!"

Indicate how you feel.   Your feelings are an important part of the message; however it is important to keep them separate from the facts. When you mix the two in your message, things can get confusing. Presenting them separately is less likely to elicit an argument. Facts stated objectively are facts, your feelings are your feelings. Indicate your feelings using words. Do not feel obligated to *express* your feelings with gestures or by raising your voice. Have confidence in the ability of your language to convey how you are feeling. Be brief and concise in describing your feelings, again remembering to focus on your own experience rather than the behavior of the other person, using "I" instead of "you."

Assertive:

"When I come across your laundry lying around, *I* feel frustrated."

Aggressive:

"When I'm surrounded by your filth, I feel like *you* don't have any respect for me, and that you have no more sense than a barnyard animal!"

Ask for what you need.   When we are unhappy with someone's behavior, we may be inclined to complain about it. When something happens that you don't like, your dissatisfaction is likely to take the initial form of a complaint in your mind. For example, you might think, "she doesn't do this enough" or "he does that too much" or "what is wrong with this person?!" You may have noticed that when you present a complaint to someone in its original complaint form, that is, the way it first occurred in your head, the other person is often less than receptive to what you have to say. One reason for this is that when complaints are directed at us, we are likely to hear them as criticism. The most natural response that human beings have to criticism is to become defensive. One way to minimize the chances of a defensive reaction is to change your complaint into a request.

There are many ways that people defend themselves when faced with a complaint. One of the most common responses is to explain how the complaint is not exactly true. Another response is to explain why one behaved in a certain way. When you change your complaint into a request, you are giving the other person the opportunity to respond by doing what you would like for them to do. If they decline to meet your request, they have the opportunity to explain why. They are not sidetracked by trying to defend themselves, which takes both of you further away from the response you are seeking.

When a complaint pops into your head, think of this as the raw material of an unmet need or wish. Before letting this raw material escape from your mouth, transform it into a format that the other person can respond to positively. Change it into a direct request. If possible, say please. For example:

Complaint:

"You never help with the dishes!"

Request:

"Could you please clear the dishes after supper?"

Try skipping directly to the third step. It's not always necessary to summarize the facts and say how you feel. Whenever possible, go directly to asking for what you need, changing your complaints into simple, direct requests. You may be surprised at how often people respond positively to this. When this doesn't work, or when you have stronger feelings about someone's behavior, then you may want to take the more comprehensive three-step approach outlined above.

Notice feelings and thoughts that get in the way. You may be tempted to forgo these suggestions when faced with feelings of anger or resentment. Often when people aggressively criticize or attack, it is based on the belief that such aggressive behavior will help them to get rid of these feelings. If you are mindful and accepting of your feelings of anger and resentment, however, you may notice that these feelings subside whether you act in an aggressive way or not. Accepting your feelings will help you to commit to acting in an assertive rather than in an aggressive way.

You may also notice certain thoughts that are barriers to asking for what you need, like "I should not have to ask" or "She should know better." Be aware that these are your personal wishes or preferences, not rules. It's okay to be aware that you do not like having to make a particular request. Notice these thoughts, but proceed with your request anyway.

Delegating Tasks

A related skill that involves being assertive and that can help anyone who tends to take on too much is the ability to delegate tasks. Delegating may be difficult if you have perfectionistic tendencies or rigid ideas about how things should be done.

Notice barriers to delegating.   For many people, delegating is accompanied by anxiety and worries about whether the task will be done right. You may have thoughts like "Nobody else will do the job as well as I would" or "It would be easier to do it myself than to show someone else how to do it." All of these are potential barriers to delegating that can be addressed using the LLAMP approach.

Start by recognizing the value of delegating certain tasks in terms of the time you will gain to pursue more highly valued activities. Even delegating one activity can make a significant difference. Practice delegating small tasks to family members and coworkers as exposure. Notice the thoughts and feelings that come up when you do this, using the LLAMP principles to develop willingness in this area.

Delegate the outcome, not the process.   If you are going to let go of a task, let go of it. Choose the right person to delegate to, and communicate what you want done. While checking in on results is fine, micromanaging the method is not really delegating.

TAKE TIME TO MASTER NEW SKILLS

Whether you are focused on improving your planning and time management, problem solving, or being more assertive, remember that developing new ways of doing things takes time. Give yourself time to improve in all of the areas discussed in this chapter. Don't toss out the calendar the first time you miss an appointment. Don't expect to find the perfect solution just because you're being more methodical about problem solving. Remember that being assertive is not a guarantee of getting what you want. Be ready for others to test your new assertiveness with some backbiting, pouting, or hostility. Remember that trying anything new is likely to be accompanied by some uncomfortable feelings and challenging thoughts. All of these offer you the opportunity to practice the skills of the LLAMP approach.

BON VOYAGE!

Hopefully, this book has helped you to more readily recognize the worry trap and to better understand how it works. Previously, finding yourself caught in this trap, you may have responded with a struggle to escape. When it comes to worry and anxiety, however, this natural, human impulse to struggle for control is part of the problem, not part of the solution. Acceptance and commitment therapy offers an alternative to control: willingness. By learning the steps of the LLAMP approach, you have started to develop the skills needed to bring this new context of willingness to your experience of worry and anxiety. Labeling worry when it occurs is the first step toward this shift in your experience. Letting go of the urge to control your feelings by leaning into them and letting go of the struggle against them will leave room for a new perspective. Accepting your thoughts and feelings as separate from yourself and separate from their referents (defusion) will give you a sense of being bigger than your worries. Mindfulness of the present moment will help to place these thoughts and feelings as part of a larger experience of which you are the observer. Finally, being clear about your values and the goals related to those values will help you to proceed in the right direction, with all of your thoughts and feelings as part of the journey.

Bon voyage!

REFERENCES

American Psychiatric Association. 1993. *Diagnostic and Statistical Manual of Mental Disorders*. 4th ed. Washington, DC: Author.

Borkovec, T.D., H. Hazlett-Stevens, and M.L. Diaz. 1999. The role of positive beliefs about worry in generalized anxiety disorder and its treatment. *Clinical Psychology and Psychotherapy* 6:126-138.

Borkovec, T.D., and J. Sides. 1979. The contribution of relaxation and expectance to fear reduction via graded imaginal exposure to feared stimuli. *Behaviour Research and Therapy* 17:529-540.

Dugas, M.J., F. Gagnon, R. Ladouceur, and M. Freeston. 1998. Generalized anxiety disorder: A preliminary test of a conceptual model. *Behaviour Research and Therapy* 36:215-226.

Foa, E.B., and M.J. Kozak. 1985. Treatment of anxiety disorders: Implications for psychopathology. In *Anxiety and the Anxiety Disorders*, edited by A.H. Tuma and J.D. Maser. Hillsdale, NJ: Erlbaum.

Hayes, S.C., S.M. McCurry, N. Afari, and K.G. Wilson. 1993. *Acceptance and Commitment Therapy: A Manual for the Treatment of Emotional Avoidance*. Reno, NV: Context Press.

Hayes, S.C., K.D. Strosahl, K. Bunting, M. Twohig, and K.G. Wilson. 2004. What is acceptance and commitment therapy? In *A Practical Guide to Acceptance and Commitment Therapy*, edited by S.C. Hayes and K.D. Strosahl. New York: Springer.

Hayes, S.C., K.D. Strosahl, and K.G. Wilson. 1999. *Acceptance and Commitment Therapy: An Experiential Approach to Behavior Change*. New York: Guilford Press.

Lang, P.J., B.G. Melamed, and J. Hart. 1970. A psychophysiological analysis of fear modification using an automated desensitization procedure. *Journal of Abnormal Psychology* 76:220-234.

Linehan, M.M., J.W. Kanter, and K.A. Comtois. 1999. Dialectical behavior therapy for borderline personality disorder: Efficacy, specificity, and cost effectiveness. In *Psychotherapy Indications and Outcomes*, edited by D.S. Janowsky. Washington, DC: American Psychiatric Press.

Metzger, R.L., M.L. Miller, M. Cohen, M. Sofka, and T.D. Borkovec. 1990. Worry changes decision-making: The effects of negative thoughts on cognitive processing. *Journal of Clinical Psychology* 46:78-88.

Premack, D. 1962. Reversibility of the reinforcement relation. *Science* 136:235-237.

Rogers, C. 1961. *On Becoming a Person: A Therapist's View of Psychotherapy*. Boston: Houghton Mifflin.

Watson, J.P., and I.M. Marks. 1971. Relevant and irrelevant fear in flooding: A crossover study of phobic patients. *Behavior Therapy* 2:275-293.

more **acceptance & commitment therapy** titles
from new**harbinger**publications

ACT ON LIFE NOT ON ANGER
The New Acceptance & Commitment Therapy
Guide to Problem Anger

$14.95 • Item Code: 4402

GET OUT OF YOUR MIND & INTO YOUR LIFE
The New Acceptance & Commitment Therapy

$19.95 • Item Code: 4259

LIVING BEYOND YOUR PAIN
Using Acceptance & Commitment Therapy
to Ease Chronic Pain

$19.95 • Item Code: 4097

THE ANOREXIA WORKBOOK
How to Accept Yourself, Heal Your Suffering
& Reclaim Your Life

$17.95 • Item Code: 3627

ACCEPTANCE & COMMITMENT THERAPY FOR ANXIETY DISORDERS
A Practitioner's Treatment Guide to Using Mindfulness,
Acceptance & Values-Based Behavior Change Strategies

$58.95 • Item Code: 4275

available from new**harbinger**publications
and fine booksellers everywhere

To order, call toll free **1-800-748-6273** or visit our online bookstore at **www.newharbinger.com**
(V, MC, AMEX • prices subject to change without notice)